Night on the Flint River

Night on the Flint River

An Accidental Journey in Knowing God

Roberta C. Bondi

Abingdon Press
Nashville

NIGHT ON THE FLINT RIVER:
AN ACCIDENTAL JOURNEY IN KNOWING GOD

Copyright © 1999 by Abingdon Press

This book is printed on recycled, acid-free, elemental-chlorine–free paper.

Library of Congress Cataloging in Publication Data

Bondi, Roberta C.
    Night on the Flint River: An Accidental Journey in Knowing God /
Roberta C. Bondi.
        p.   cm.
    ISBN 0-687-02455-2 (alk. paper)
    1. Bondi, Roberta C.   2. Christian biography—United States.
3. Canoes and canoeing—Georgia—Flint River. 4. Flint River (Ga.)—
Description and travel.   I. Title.
BR1725.B62A3   1999
230'.044'092—dc21
[b]   99-19063
                                                                CIP

Scripture quotations, unless otherwise indicated, are from the New
Revised Standard Version Bible, copyright © 1989, by the Division of
Christian Education of the National Council of the Churches of Christ
in the United States of America.

Scripture quotations noted RSV are from the Revised Standard Version
of the Bible, copyright 1946, 1952, 1971 by the Division of Christian
Education of the National Council of the Churches of Christ in the USA.
Used by permission.

99 00 01 02 03 04 05 06 07 08—10 9 8 7 6 5 4 3 2 1

MANUFACTURED IN THE UNITED STATES OF AMERICA

To Richard

Contents

Preface

The following is the story of an adventure that took place not too many years ago. Pam and I and our friend Jeff had gone out intending to take a short, simple, and relaxing Sunday afternoon canoe trip on the Flint River not very far from Atlanta. Nothing turned out as we expected, however, and before long we were in trouble. There had been a drought some time before, which had killed many trees. Almost as soon as we were in the water we found ourselves entangled among their dead trunks, roots, and branches that had fallen across the river. Having decided, in spite of the obvious, to push on in hope of finding that the water would be clear farther along, within hours we were in total darkness, the likes of which I, at least, had never known before. During the long hours till the dawn that followed, I truly believed that I was living out the last night of my life. This book recounts not just what happened to us on that October 18, but also something of my interior reflections as I stumbled along in the wet blackness with my two friends, expecting to die.

As for these reflections, I have learned from experience that when something happens to me that puts me in a place of danger, delight, beauty, loss, illness, accident, or pain that is as far from my ordinary experience as this night was, I need to pay attention, and to pay that attention in the presence of God. When I do, I learn things and receive gifts that I am generally aware I can learn and receive no other way. Make no mistake, however. I am not suggesting that God deliberately caused what occurred that night in order to teach me a lesson. It was our own stubborn refusal to turn back once it became obvious that the deadfalls in the Flint River were not going to go away that got us stranded. I do believe, however, that when something like this happens to any of us, if we are attentive and honest with ourselves, God is able to use these times that seem to set us so at the boundaries between life and death, mystery and the ordinary, to speak to us in ways that help us grow in love of God and neighbor.

At the same time, if we are talking about bone-jarring events and the long-term growth in love, paying attention while the crisis is taking place and remembering in detail what happened later in the presence of God in our prayer is only one part of what we need to do in order to make ourselves available to receive God's gifts.

For myself, I am aware that I also need to treat that first occasion not as an event that has taken place and is now over, but rather as the beginning point for the kind of reflection in the loving and challenging presence of God that will make it possible for me to bring the whole of myself—mind, heart, experience, my awareness of my culture, my knowledge of the early church and its life and theology, which I study and teach, and scripture— into transforming conversation with the original happening. This is not fast work. It often takes a very long time, sometimes even years, and it is frequently painful; but when it comes to transformation into love of God and neighbor, I have found it is always worth the patient and continued effort.

It is hardly surprising, if I consider our common identity in Christ, as well as our common calling to growth in love, that though sometimes this work must be private, more often than not, I usually benefit greatly from sharing this conversation with Christian friends, as I also benefit from their sharing equivalent conversations with me. Certainly, such shared talk in turn helps all of us as the body of Christ truly to encounter our loving God as well as to think more clearly and honestly about who we actually are both individually and as God's people.

It is in this spirit and with these intentions, at any rate, that I offer to you my own reflections around that night with God and my friends on the Flint River three years ago. I hope you may use the record of this conversation to spark your own thoughts and prayers around your experiences, metaphorically speaking, of the wilderness through which sooner or later all of us must go.

Here, before I begin, I want to thank some people who made this project possible.

To begin, there is my friend Pam Couture, who was with me that night. She has moved out of Atlanta, and I miss dreadfully her fun, her intelligence, and her general enthusiasm for life. I also want to thank our other companion that October 18, Jeff Smith, for his stoic patience in the face of his injury.

I also particularly want to thank Candler School of

Preface

Theology, where I teach, for giving me a study leave in which to write this book.

Halfway through the composition of *Night on the Flint River,* as I was coming down the hill from our neighbors' house during a severe rainstorm, I fell on some rocks and shattered my ankle. Here, I want to express my gratitude to my friends who dragged me through the wilderness of a week in the hospital, surgery, three and a half months in a cast, and the following months of physical therapy as I wrote. Maggie Kulyk, Melissa Walker, and Caroline Walker Bynum were particularly heroic, as was my mother, Mary Cowan.

At the same time, I can also hardly imagine getting through the event of my ankle so that I could write about the Flint River without my other friends who, among other things, brought food, visited, carted me around, talked on the phone and made me laugh. Some of these, but certainly not all, include Tere Canzoneri, Marian Dolan, Wendy Farley, Kim Frndak, Carl Hall, Elaine LaLonde, Bill and Gatra Mallard, Nicole Mills, Bobbi Patterson, Michelle Rubin, Don Saliers, Elaine Stenovsky, and Peggy West.

Most of all, however, I want to thank my husband, Richard, the person who, when I was laid up in the cast all those months, cared for me the most. He is always my best, most supportive, and most challenging conversation partner. I am very sorry that this adventure was the source of his flattened curls, hollow eyes, and lined forehead, which, for two whole weeks after my night on the Flint River, made him look as though he had an unspeakable migraine headache. May he never have to go through such a time again!

Chapter 1

Beginnings

I have to face it: I am simply not an outdoor person. I had always thought I was, however, before that black night I spent with Pam and Jeff, lost on the Flint River, one of the longest rivers in Georgia.

Growing up in cities, some of my most wondrous childhood memories had come from finding myself in the outdoors, if only briefly, in places far from home. I never forgot the look and feel of the snow-dusted brown mountains of the Adirondacks, for example, where my family went one year to spend Thanksgiving with my step-great-grandmother. I was let out of the car for a moment, once, to stretch my arms and get some air to fight the motion sickness that always accompanied my father's chain smoking while he drove. Even now I feel as a deep vibration in my chest the peculiar way the slopes of the mountains flowed down so steeply to the crumbled, dry, leaf-covered edges of the narrow road.

For the rest of that day, once we had arrived at our destination, the adults talked and laughed endlessly about things I couldn't understand in the enormous, high-ceilinged, faded living room of the old woman I barely knew. Did we eat? It was Thanksgiving, so I suppose we surely must have. What I remember instead of eating, however, is my own silence. There was nothing in that place of ancient manners and mannered conversation that I was able to say, or was allowed to say, or wanted to say.

Instead, I sat by the fire, half bored, half angry, imagining myself, a child, wandering alone in those dark mountains I had just passed through, mountains I shared only with a mysterious, benevolent presence whom I did not name, thick-coated black bears browsing and growling through the underbrush, and deer, antlered and quick as I would have liked to be, their feet neatly tucked under their shining bodies as they leaped around me through the leafless black thickets in which they lived.

For years I dreamed almost deliriously of being lost to all grown-ups on the slopes of those low winter mountains. They were freedom to me, beauty and silence on my own terms, and also mystery. They stood for a world in which I absolutely believed, though I could barely see it, a world both larger and smaller than my own imagination. Later, as a confused, disoriented young woman, even a momentary memory of the look of those foreshortened mountains could bring me face to face with the solidity of my own interior landscapes, while in the same instant that very memory confronted me paradoxically with the wondrous, absolutely unknowable alienness of all that was not me.

My experience of the outdoors as I camped with Richard in the first years we were married was, in some ways, a fulfilling of my childhood imaginings. Certainly, it was very deeply nourishing, and even healing. As a little girl I had longed to escape into the wilderness from the pressures of the adult world in which I could not find a place for myself or words to speak. As a woman worn out from the pervasive internal and external stresses of trying to hold up my head, pray, and work in what was still a largely male academic environment, those early camping trips gave me much of the sense of a place and words of my own I had so wanted as a child.

Still, in other ways, my adult life in the outdoors on these early camping trips was very different from my childhood vision of those mountains. For one thing, there was very little genuine wildness to it, because we rarely camped in uncivilized places. Though we loved to pretend we were in the wilderness, as we ate, washed, and slept without a roof over our heads, during those first years, when the children were small, we always pitched our tents with other families among the bushes and pine trees on the flat, tamped-down pads of dirt provided for that purpose by the state parks of Georgia. We canoed and fished in the morning mist and later watched the sun set over rippling pink and silver water, and it was beautiful. Still, we cooked on the stove we brought with us, obliterated the darkness within the circle of our picnic table with gas lanterns, and slept on the floor of our tent in sleek sleeping bags, which were lighter than down and twice as warm. The next morning, we showered in warm bathhouses, dried ourselves with thick towels, and dressed in clean clothes.

Later, as Grace and Benjamin grew older and more

unwilling to leave the telephone, the refrigerator, and their other teen-age amusements, and Richard and I grew more tired, sore, and busy, we abandoned even the little wildness that sleeping on the ground had afforded us. We decided that what we needed most was comfort, a chance simply to get away, to rest, and to be at peace. We bought a pop-up, a kind of cross between a small house trailer and a tent to be towed behind the car. From then on, we could camp at the same time we and our disgruntled children could sleep in real beds, cook and eat indoors, out of the weather. On nice weekends in spring and summer we could haul the pop-up out to Stone Mountain Park, not twenty minutes from home, and set up.

There, in the middle of the day while the children tirelessly talked on the pay phones (if they had not already arranged to spend the night with friends), Richard fished, and I prayed and did my work peacefully on the kitchen table of our playhouse, preparing for classes, reading texts, grading papers, and writing on my portable computer. Early mornings and evenings we still walked through the campgrounds telling silly stories, our boots scuffing up leathery bottles of wild ginger beneath our feet. We squinted at the shore of the lake for a glimpse of the two blue herons who had their nest there. We sniffed the good smells of coffee, bacon, hamburgers, or marshmallows cooking at our neighbors' campsites. We slept, dry and warm, to the sound of rain rattling on the roof of the pop-up above our heads. It was delightfully comfortable.

Soon the children grew up, went off to school, and moved away. Though Richard and I continued to have some good times in our pop-up out at Stone Mountain—

tired as we were from our busy weeks, we still didn't get more adventurous or go farther from home in those years—we didn't camp as much as we used to. Richard had begun training for a new profession and had very little spare time, and while in theory I pined for the outdoors, increasingly I found myself doing so much traveling that camping became more of a chore than a pleasure.

I missed it dreadfully. I was not so raw and sore as I had once been. The wounds of my childhood and young adulthood were mostly healed. My life, too, as an academic woman had become easier as I established a place for myself at school and found a way of doing my own work that was congenial to me. My writing as well as my comings and goings, however, had also grown more complex, and I longed for the quiet and rest of those earlier days and nights in the familiar campground. I still needed those old weekends in which I could blot out the world, go to bed among tall, straight trees with the smell of pine needles in my nose, get up in the morning and go out paddling the canoe with Richard on a lake as smooth and cool as a mirror.

At the same time, oddly, as I continued to long for the peace and safety I had experienced in those earlier times, I realized that my childhood vision of the alien outdoors was coming back. I began to long again for the undomesticated, unknowable wilderness of my younger imagination, a wilderness of bears and deer, and, above all, God.

It is hardly surprising, then, that when Pam telephoned, one evening toward the beginning of October three years ago, I was willing to listen to her proposal. She wanted to invite me to go with her and our mutual friend Jeff on a short Sunday afternoon canoe trip on the Flint River. I knew immediately that I should turn her down. If I were to accept her invitation, between the time she called and the afternoon in question two weeks later I would have been out of town three different times, in addition to my regular teaching. I was already exhausted, and I hadn't even packed my suitcase for my first trip. I told Pam I would like to go, but it seemed impossible. Still, she pounced immediately on the real regret she heard in my voice.

"Oh no," said Pam. "Of course it's not impossible. We'll make it good for you; I know you're tired. I intend to park Jeff's van at one end of the stretch we'll be floating down, at an old mill, then drive the car to a point up the river where we'll put in the canoe. You won't have to do anything but sit between us on the floor of the boat while Jeff and I paddle. You'll be in the canoe an hour, two hours, at the most, then we'll get out at the mill, get the van, and go back for the car. There'll be nothing to it. I read about it in a book on easy canoe trips in Georgia. The book says the river is beautiful after we pass a few deadfalls right after we put the boat in the water. Doesn't that sound nice?"

Well, it did and it didn't. On the one hand, whatever I ended up doing, I knew perfectly well that nothing planned by Pam, herself a veritable force of nature, could possibly be as restful as spending an afternoon in bed tucked up under my maroon comforter, napping, snacking, drinking hot tea, and recovering for the next week's work.

On the other hand, Pam is so dear and full of enthusiasm for outdoor trips of all kinds (she actually likes to go camping in the snow!), so generous, and so innocent in her desire to share her pleasure with her friends that it had always been hard for me to decline her offers, no matter what she proposed. In addition, it had been a long time since Richard's and my last camping trip, and I knew that my upcoming travel schedule made another trip unlikely for a good long while. The idea of gliding smoothly down a shining but abandoned stretch of an October river beneath the bare, intricate branches of overhanging trees sounded nearly irresistible.

Pam interrupted my slightly panicky deliberations. "Please?" she said. I pictured her dark brown eyes laughing in her mischievous face on the other end of the line, and I gave up. Absolutely against my better judgment I said yes.

When the day came, I was as wrung out from traveling as I had expected. It had been raining steadily in Atlanta for the four days before we were scheduled to go. I have to admit, I had hoped to wake up to such a blinding storm that our trip would have to be canceled. Unfortunately for me, it was already obvious that morning that the weather was clearing. The radio by our bed confirmed what I could see for myself: watery sunlight was visible above the tops of our bedroom shutters. The unwelcome voice of the announcer promised typical Georgia October temperatures for the rest of the day, cold in the morning and evening, hot in the afternoon.

As I lay there beside the warm body of my husband, I was only able to groan at what was now obvious: I would have to go, but I could hardly sit up. Richard did what he could for me. He loves to be out on the water; imagining an idyllic trip on a peaceful river, he was disappointed that he would have to stay behind and work on textbook orders in the bookstore. He patted me gently, promising to meet us upon our return with a pot of homemade soup and bread, and I hugged him gratefully. A few minutes later he got up, made me a pot of coffee, and brought it to me, cup by cup, along with a handful of vitamins. Loaded with coffee as I finally dragged my aching body out of bed, I tripped over my packed suitcase, stood a good long time in a hot shower, then dressed myself in an old purple sweat suit I'd borrowed from Richard.

Clothed at last, I couldn't imagine how I would physically get through this trip. I suppose it could have been this sense of the impossibility of what lay ahead of me that produced what I might have taken for an omen if Christians believed in them. That morning as I had stood in the shower, steaming water running over my hurting head and my sore shoulders, all of a sudden a thought had flashed through my mind like an announcement heard on the radio by the bed: "Today is the last day of my life."

Now, as I said, I don't put any stock in omens—not being St. Anthony or one of the other ancient desert teachers who were so free of their passions that they could see the future—nor did I really think I had been given a glimpse into what was to come. What my own brain had spoken to me was nothing more than an interesting possibility. I took it seriously, but I was not frightened, and it certainly did not seem to me to constitute a reason to abandon the trip ahead of me. I was tired and a little desperate, but I had given Pam my word, and I was too proud to tell her I needed to break it. Besides, I could not bring myself to disappoint her by backing out at the last minute.

By the time Pam and Jeff drove up the driveway at 11:00 A.M., physically I was feeling marginally better, anyway. The two of them, dressed for a warm fall day of boating on an easy river, were full of themselves, joking about something that had gone on at church on the previous weekend. After one more quick cup of coffee with Richard and me, they hoisted our old green canoe from the saw horses by the garage and strapped it on the top of Jeff's van. We collected the paddles and the life preservers. Pam already had a map in her book on Georgia. None of us worried about food, water, or other supplies, though Richard stuck two high-energy bars in my raincoat pocket at the last minute. What else could we need? Though we would be driving for a while before we arrived at the place where we would put in our canoe, we certainly did not intend to be on the water more than an hour or two. We would pick up a fast lunch and a few junk food snacks to take with us for the afternoon in the nearest town before we launched.

At least in its physical aspects, the first part of the trip went pretty much as Pam had promised. We drove in tandem through town and out into the autumn countryside, Pam and I in the car and Jeff in the van, to the little town closest to where we would launch. When we got there, we had a mild squabble over where to eat lunch. Pam and Jeff were both on low-fat diets, as I ought to have been, but I was certain that sitting passively in the bottom of the canoe would take protein, and they decided to humor me. I was feeling guilty about getting my way and we were all a bit out of sorts, but we agreed on barbeque at a place with a screened-in porch for eating on in the summer. The sweet-smelling smoke rose from a chimney behind it like prayers and incense and made my mouth water.

The indoor room was full of smokers, which I didn't like, and waitresses who called everybody "hon" and "sugar," which I did. The pork was tasty, tender, and tangy in its Georgia sauce, as full of grease and salty as it ought to have been. We filled our stomachs with it along with bowls of Brunswick stew as we talked lazily about what was coming next. Then, satisfied in mind and body, we stopped at the gas station next door for a large bag of salty pretzels and a sack of nourishing red licorice to take with us. After some minor debate, since we didn't like the idea of carrying the weight, we also decided that we ought to add a gallon-sized plastic jug of drinking water.

A half hour later we had found the old mill and parked the car. Before the three of us climbed back into the van we had a walk on the grounds, stretching our legs and enjoying the rapidly warming air. The food in our stomachs, the spacious canopy of brown and yellow foliage above our heads, and the thick layer of wet black leaves beneath our feet filled us with contentment. Nothing that lay ahead of us felt particularly ominous or even arduous, and all of us, even I, fortified as I was with good greasy barbeque, left the mill basking in hope and ready to drive the ten miles up the road to look for what we assumed would be our well-marked launching spot.

When I think back on it now, it seems to me that it was at this point when we began our frustrating search for our entry to the river that we should have begun to have an inkling of what might lie ahead of us. For a long time we could not find where we were to go; we were only able to see the small, nearly invisible sign that signaled our put-in place after we had driven past it six or eight times with our necks craned. When we found it at last, it was well hidden in the thorny bushes by the water's edge at the bottom of a long, steep, very soggy-looking ditch that paralleled the stretch of two-lane highway we had been back and forth on so many times already.

To try to park in that ditch was to take our lives in our hands, but there was nothing else to do. Taking as long and slow a running start as we could at the shallowest place we could find, we eased into the bottom of it without turning over. Already grunting and sweating, we stumbled around in the muck as we lifted down the canoe. We locked up at last, collected our stuff, and started off to find the path, carefully picking up our feet, which made great sucking noises as we walked. We were greatly relieved to have gotten over what was certain to be the hump of our trip. We only figured to carry the boat a short distance through the prickly, gray-green bushes that edged the still invisible water ahead of us.

It took us longer to reach the river than we expected. By now, dragging the canoe along the narrow path that had begun to show itself at the edge of the underbrush, we came upon a grizzly sight that stopped us where we stood. Lying by the bushes in the shadows next to our feet was the mangled, half-desiccated carcass of a small deer. Whether it had been shot by a bullet or an illicit arrow or been brought down by a pack of wild dogs wasn't immediately apparent. It might have died of some dreadful disease or even starvation. Who knows? It was obvious that it had died horribly. Its body had been eaten away by something; there was nothing left of it but the half dried remains of its poor reddish brown head, the skinny bottom parts of four legs of moth-eaten velvet, and its small dark hooves.

Setting the canoe down in the soft dirt beneath our feet, we stared at its remains and tried to make sense of what we were seeing.

Pam was the one who broke the silence. "Whoa," she said, scuffing a high-topped canvas tennis shoe in the dirt of the path beside her. "Something bad happened here!" Always interested in everything, she handed me her jacket as she squatted down, bright-eyed, to take a closer look.

Jeff shifted back and forth on his feet next to her. I don't remember his reply as he stood there, just his tone of voice and the fact that he made the sort of joke people make when they are anxious and they can't escape their own anxiety. Nor do I recall my own answer, if there was one, only my horror and my physical dread in the presence of this innocent animal's death. I gazed at the defenseless little pile of bones, dirty fur, and crusted feet lying in the bedraggled grass before me, with my legs weak and my stomach churning. Then, all at once the phrase I'd already heard myself speak in the shower that morning spoke again in my head like a voice from heaven: "This is the last day of my life."

"This is the last day of my life." It is one thing to speak these words from the safety of a warm shower, another altogether when you are staring at the body of a dead animal lying on the ground in front of you. I could afford to ignore these words in the morning, figuring that they must surely be no more than the sound of my own exhaustion. I still didn't believe in omens, nor do I now; nevertheless, I took note and paid attention, though, never having experienced anything like this before, I was hardly prepared to identify what paying attention might actually mean or to whom I was attending.

("Yes, it is true," St. Anthony used to say back in the fourth-century Egyptian desert when everyone still took the existence of demons for granted; "sometimes the demons really do know what is about to happen and they can tell you what it will be. This does not mean, however, that they can predict the future through supernatural powers and therefore should either be respected or feared. It is only that they have very, very light and thin bodies, and so they can run so amazingly fast that they are able to go on the trail ahead of the monks, see what is about to happen, and run back to tell the gullible what they have seen. The best thing to do when faced with such a situation is simply to ignore them.")

"This is the last day of my life." I wasn't about to repeat what had once more crossed my mind to my companions, and I didn't want to stand around dithering about it any longer, either. I turned my head away. "Let's go," I said as I gave my arm to Pam so that she could pull herself to her feet. Without further reference to the gruesome remains of the deer, we picked up the boat and went off to find our launching place.

Once through the thicket, we saw that the river was much narrower and shallower than Pam's book had led us to expect. Still, the bank was muddy, cool, and sweet with sparse green grass, and the surface of the water invitingly dappled with sunlight. We found a place easily enough to set the canoe in the water; then we tossed our jackets, snacks, the canoe guide, my backpack, and the water bottle onto its sturdy cream-colored bottom and climbed in. In no time at all we had set off for the bend in the river that was just visible ahead of us.

The next five minutes were as lovely as we had hoped. At last, we were able to relax completely. The mirrored water around us dimpled with tiny eddies, and the air was warm and full of the good smell of slippery wet leaves and black earth from the four days of storm that had preceded our trip. The branches of the bare trees in the woods around us dripped big drops of old rain in which the sun winked and whispered. On the floor between Pam and Jeff as they paddled, I sat cross-legged on a thin pad I'd stowed in my backpack. I imagined Jeff's big knees sticking up above my head and his rugged face grinning behind me as Pam began to sing some silly song in front. Tired or not, I was glad I had come; it would be a good trip. Sighing with pleasure, I closed my eyes and trailed the tips of my fingers in the shining water on either side of the boat, my own paddle, unused, beside me.

Pam stopped singing. "Okay," she called out a moment later. "Everybody alert! It's time to go around the bend."

I drew in my hands, made the effort to open my eyes, and dropped my mouth open in astonishment. What lay ahead of us looked nothing like where we'd been five minutes before.

The new landscape had entirely lost its look of peaceful hospitality. Now, we were in a wilderness quite unlike the safe wild places of my childhood fantasy. We were entering a world that seemed to have been shaped by some sort of natural disaster. The river, which appeared suddenly both to have narrowed sharply and lost most of its water, ran through a winter woods that had been made a blackened swamp by the preceding days' rains. Its banks were uneven, full of holes and hills tangled with thick, thorny blackberry bushes and bits of abandoned barbed-wire fence. Big slippery-looking trees with bent-over backs leaned against each other beside the water and glowered, their limbs broken half through at odd angles far above our heads.

Then there were the deadfalls. When you are canoeing, a deadfall is a tree that has died or been hit by lightning and fallen over into the water, and that is what there were so many of, that afternoon on the Flint River, that we couldn't see the end of them. Every few feet, there was a tree, bare of leaves but prolifically branched, lying entirely across the river, its dead and naked roots rising several feet in the air on one bank, its bedraggled crown on the other, with the main body of its branches above and below the water in between.

"Look at this," I cried out, dismayed and frightened by the very sight of so much incomprehensible devastation. My stomach hurt as the muscles in my thighs cramped up. "There is no possible way we can get through this. We'll just have to turn around right here and go back."

It was a waste of good breath. Pam loves the difficult. She was already out of the canoe and standing in the shallow water beside it. I could feel the boat rock as behind me Jeff got ready to follow her.

"No way are we going back," she answered me. "I told you the book said there were a few deadfalls at the beginning. After that, though—only a little after that—the water is supposed to be clear. We can't possibly quit now. The guide says this is one of the most beautiful stretches on the Flint River."

I looked around me dubiously. I couldn't imagine how the river could ever come to fit the book's description if we followed it for ten miles. Even that it lose a little of its bleakness seemed impossible from where I stood.

Pam walked back beside me and stuck out a hand while I was still trying to think up an unanswerable reply that would satisfy her and get us all out of there. "Come on," she said. "Out you go, old creaky; we can't carry the boat over that tree in front of us. There's nothing to do but find a place to portage."

Automatically, I took her hand and hoisted myself up, my backpack over one shoulder, my paddle in my hand. How could we portage when the bank was so high and the underbrush so thick?

"Pam, we can't do it," I said again, desperately. By now I was standing beside her in the water, trying to see a place we might carry the canoe around the tree, should all of us be so inclined.

"Of course we can," she answered. "I've canoed in

much worse places than this. I know what we can do." At this, she turned to Jeff, who had still not said anything. "Jeff, tell her we can do it."

Jeff, who, as a former athlete, is both taciturn and proud of his toughness, nodded his head. He looked at me and smiled. "Of course we can," he said. He picked up his end of the canoe with one huge hand while Pam picked up hers. The two of them started walking through the water toward the right bank, which was graced with a long patch of mud we could probably carry the canoe across.

I hurried to catch up with Pam to do my share at her end. "Now, don't complain," she said as she turned her head to look at me. Her face was lit with pleasure; my friend was entirely in her element. "Did I tell you about the alligators we saw on the river south of Macon? You have to be tough when you go on a canoe trip!"

I thought longingly of my soft bed and my mystery novel at home and sneaked a sigh. I should have known better than to have come. Maybe I was wrong about what was ahead of us, however, and if I were, how could I spoil Pam's and Jeff's trip by insisting on going back now?

"Okay," I answered out loud. "I'll be as tough as I need to be."

Pam nodded her approval. "Good girl," she said.

Fifteen or twenty deadfalls later, however, the river still had not cleared. We had paddled the short distances between them when we were able. More significant, we had portaged a few more times; but more often than we had carried the boat overland we had stood in the shallow water dragging, lifting, and pushing the canoe through, over, and under the branches of the deadfalls. Worn out before we even started, by now my back and arms were killing me, my stomach hurt, my mouth was excruciatingly dry, and my legs were shaking.

I looked at my watch; it was four o'clock. Richard would be expecting us back in Atlanta for supper in only two hours. What would he think had happened if we didn't show up? For some reason, I was reluctant to bring Richard into it.

"We need to go back," I said. "We'll never get through this way" (which was true). "It's going to get dark" (which was also true).

"What do you mean?" asked Pam. "We can't go back now," said Jeff. They looked at me with surprise.

"Why not?" I wanted to know. There really seemed to me to be no other reasonable option open to us, after all.

"Because I'm sure we're already much closer to the mill where we take out the boat than we are to the place where we put the canoe in the water," Jeff said.

Pam added, "Because the river *has* to get clear soon; the book says it does. We *can't* go back till we find the good parts of the river. That's what we came for." Her expressive face was pleading with me.

I crossed my arms across my mud-covered chest and looked as stubborn as I could muster. "I don't think it is going to clear up any time soon," I said, "and furthermore, even though we've been out two or three hours by now, I'm positive we haven't come more than a mile or two from where we started."

We were at a standstill; we looked at each other in consternation. What were we to do? I knew that if I insisted, Pam and Jeff would turn around and humor me as they had at lunch; but I didn't want to insist, and, even now, I especially didn't want to disappoint Pam.

Inside myself I began backing down. Perhaps, I told myself, things were not as bad as I thought. Maybe I was only being crotchety because I was so tired.

"Okay," I said at last, though my heart had sunk through the soaking wet legs of my borrowed purple sweat suit right through to the soles of my wrinkled-up feet; "let's keep going."

Pam beamed, delighted, and came to give me a hug. "Let's have a snack before we go on," she said. She squinted her eyes and looked at me critically. "What you need is some food." Pam pulled out the sack of red licorice and popped open the bag of pretzels and passed them around. We were all hungry. We stuffed our mouths with the chewy stuff and the crunchy stuff; then, thirsty from the sugar and salt, we washed down everything with water from our plastic jug. After that, we started up again through the dark woods and the pale light.

It was only about an hour later, when the sun was clearly on its way down, that we finally hit our first truly insurmountable problem. Pam and I were paddling slowly through one of the rare open spaces on the shallow river while Jeff walked ahead of the canoe to see what was coming up in front of us. Without warning, Jeff stopped still in the water, his body rigid. We could tell immediately that something was very wrong.

"What's the matter, Jeff?" we asked together, bringing the canoe alongside him.

"Twisted my knee and ripped the cartilage in it," he gasped out between teeth clenched with pain.

"How do you know?" Pam questioned, anxiously.

Jeff closed his eyes and reached down slowly to feel around on his wounded joint. "I've done it enough times in my running days; I know what it is," he said.

"How can we help?" I asked next.

"Nothing for it but surgery when we get back," he answered in a near whisper. "Maybe if I can get in the canoe, the two of you can paddle me."

It was obvious to me that this wasn't going to work for more than a few feet, until we came to the next dead tree, but I was happy to try that far. Bracing himself with his hands on our shoulders, Jeff somehow lowered himself into the back of the boat and sat with his leg stuck straight out in front of him. Immediately, we could feel him withdraw into himself to manage the pain. Pam and I looked at each other with frustration; soon he would have to walk. Neither of us mentioned the impending darkness.

Pam got back into the boat to paddle, and I waded along beside her until we came to the next deadfall. By now Jeff was absolutely white and totally silent. No way could we expect him to climb out of the boat and drag himself over or around the fallen tree. There was nothing to do except for Pam and me to go right through its branches. We looked for a place we thought we could manage, the two of us prying away limbs, pulling them up, and pushing them down again as they snapped in our faces until we got the canoe through them with Jeff in it. Once on the other side I, at least, was so tired I hardly knew what to do. I couldn't make this effort again. In spite of my best intentions, from this point on, Jeff would have to find a way to walk while Pam and I handled the boat.

And this is what we did for another hour as the sun ominously continued to sink. Without further conversation, at the next deadfall Jeff used his paddle as a crutch to drag himself out of the water and up onto the left bank. Pam and I continued as we had before, occasionally stealing glances at the silent figure clad only in muddy shorts and a T-shirt propping himself on his makeshift cane as he slowly walked above us.

It was sometime during this last hour after Jeff's injury, as the light began to fail in earnest and the temperature began to drop, that for the third time that day the thought crossed my mind, "This is the last day of my life." This time, in the presence of those words, I stopped in my tracks. Under the circumstances in which I now found myself with my friends, I could no longer write them off as merely a slightly hysterical response to my own exhaustion.

"This is the last day of my life." All of a sudden, I knew it really was. I *was* going to die that night on the Flint River, and maybe Pam and Jeff would die with me. There was no "perhaps" to it, no point of negotiation with God or with reality. It was a fact. Death might come by accident, a fall, drowning (though this would have to be worked at in the shallow water), hypothermia, or snakebite. More probably, one or more of us would die by a bullet. Though we had passed no houses nor seen any other human beings, as the afternoon wore on, increasingly we had heard the sounds of the shotguns and rifles of hunters; we would likely be drunkenly mistaken for deer and shot. No matter, any of it. As a result of Jeff's injury, we couldn't get him back over and around the deadfalls; and with darkness falling, even if the river were suddenly to clear, it would soon be equally impossible to go forward.

Very oddly, considering that as a child death was an ongoing terror to me, and that this terror persisted well into my middle adult years as well, it is amazing that my dominant emotion through the whole of those utterly black and nearly starless hours that followed was not fear. I knew I was going to die and I was not afraid. When consuming wet blackness fell on our heads from the sky and welled up from the ground around our feet and legs, I still was unafraid even as we abandoned the canoe. We could no longer see to try to walk along a treacherously tangled bank of an indistinguishable river that, like our hands before our faces, was completely, perfectly invisible. I was going to die without rescue; why wasn't I afraid?

When Julian of Norwich was young, she tells us in *Showings*—her own account of the revelations she received over a short period of time when she was thirty and her several-year-long theological reflections on them—she asked God for three gifts. One of these was that in the future she would have such an illness that she would truly think she was going to die of it without actually dying, so that she could go through all that would immediately precede her death, experience it, practice it, learn from it and be blessed by it. At the same time, she asked for the gift of what she called "compassion" in order that she be able to share in and so understand the sufferings of Jesus.

Long after she had forgotten what she had asked for, God gave her what she had desired. In her thirtieth year, Julian became so dreadfully ill that she and those who loved her were convinced that she was dying. She was given last rites in her little anchorhold beside the church at Norwich. Her flesh appeared to fail for two more days and nights. Then when it seemed that her body was "dead from the middle downward," a priest came to her and held up a crucifix before her face so that she could focus her eyes on it as she died. Though her interior sight was already fixed on heaven, reluctantly, she wrenched herself away and did as she was asked, and as she looked on, all the light seemed to disappear from the room except that which fell immediately on the cross before her.

Suddenly, Julian tells us, her pain ceased and she felt perfectly healthy, though she did not yet believe that she would live. Then Julian remembered the prayer she had prayed so many years earlier, that God would allow her lovingly and compassionately to share in the pains of Jesus, and she asked again. Immediately, she says:

> I saw the red blood trickling down from under the crown, all hot, flowing freely and copiously, a living stream, just as it seemed to me that it was at the time when the crown of thorns was thrust down upon his blessed head. Just so did he, both God and man, suffer for me. I perceived, truly and powerfully, that it was himself who showed this

to me, without any intermediary; and then I said: Blessed be the Lord![1]

This was the beginning of the first of Julian's sixteen visions, revelations, and conversations with Jesus on which she meditated theologically for twenty years or more before she wrote the long version of her *Showings* as it has come down to us who love her.

Make no mistake. I am no Julian. Julian would have been an extraordinary person in any time. She was a brilliant, amazingly articulate, and fearless woman, who during that short period of her revelations not only saw God and lived, she talked to Jesus and Jesus talked to her in return. She was a saint to whom God gave a deeper and more radical sense of God's love than to any other human being I have ever known or read, and God gave her such a sense, according to her own testimony, not for herself alone, but for the upbuilding of all God's people.

I could never be Julian. Still, over my years of prayer, I have become convinced that it is not to such a saint alone that God gives such gifts as she received, but also to ordinary people like us who teach, practice the flute, do the laundry, and carry out the garbage. To us, too, God reveals Godself as we need God and are able to pay attention to receive God. God picks us up out of our everyday view of things only to set us down again for a little while so that we may see the world, the people around us, and

1. *Julian of Norwich: Showings*, trans., Edmund Colledge, O.S.A. and James Walsh, S.J., Classics of Western Spirituality (Mahwah, N.J.: Paulist Press, 1978).

even something of the mystery of God's self from the place of God's own compassionate vision.

Now, I have no memory at all of having asked God explicitly, as Julian had, that I might find myself in a wild landscape where I would believe I was about to die without actually going through the dying. Knowing my own fear of death over the years, I can't imagine that I could have ever made such a request. Still, perhaps it was not my prayer at all but Julian's, which she prayed for me in the communion of the saints, that God answered in that place where everything was exposed roots, wetness, and impenetrable darkness. Considering not only my fear but my longing to look more deeply on the mystery of God, I certainly needed this very thing Julian asked for herself. At any rate, it was given to me that night on the Flint River, not as it was to Julian but in a form and shape far less exalted and much more suited to my own peculiarities (Jesus never spoke a word to me or once showed me his face). God gave me what I needed as surely as God filled Julian's need on her bed in her little hut in Norwich so many centuries ago.

That I should understand this trip to be a gift of God sounds like an odd statement from a twentieth-century person who absolutely does not believe that all that happens to us is a happy result of God's will. If I did, how could I explain the dreadful deaths of little children too young to learn from their experience, of plane crashes, war, and famine? But let me tell you more about what happened in that wilderness, and something of my later reflections on God that came from it, and you can judge for yourself where God's hand actually was in it.

Chapter 2

Leaving the Canoe

W e had been walking, dragging, lifting, and carrying for close to seven hours when night suddenly began to fall—at least it felt sudden to me. I wasn't paying attention to the time; I had been putting the whole of the little energy I had left into pulling, pushing, and every now and then paddling the canoe through the increasingly impenetrable mess of roots, branches, and withered foliage in the river and around it. I really hadn't wanted to be measuring the density of the gray light visible in the sky every few minutes. What good would that have done? It was very clear to me that we were not about to leave the wilderness before it got dark.

For some time, now, it had been just one foot before the other for all three of us. Jeff with his torn knee continued to parallel Pam and me on the impossible bank above us, sometimes ahead of us, sometimes behind. In his flimsy shorts and muddy T-shirt, slowly and stoically, like a zombie, or rather like a wounded and crazed wildcat stalking something he couldn't possibly bring down, he had been ripping and staggering through the blackberry vines and bushes of the soaked underbrush and over the slippery trees. Having completely withdrawn into himself by this time to escape the pain in his leg, he did not talk to us.

Pam had also been quiet, though her quietness was of a different order than Jeff's. Indoors, Pam has always been a talker when need be; outdoors, her natural state is extroverted, alert silence. I was certain that she was tired; with her need to feel strong and in control of her physical circumstances, however, I would not have dreamed of asking her. I had no idea what she had been thinking the last hour or so; optimist that she was, she almost certainly hadn't been making an assessment of her past life or thinking through what would happen to her nearest and dearest as a result of her death. In her turquoise and purple rain suit and high-topped canvas shoes, she was by far the least bedraggled of the three of us. Still, when she turned to me in the failing light, I could see that the legs of her pants and the arms of her jacket were smeared in mud and wet leaves, and her cheeks were streaked in the same dirt that must have marked my own. Tired as she had to have been, she was certainly present enough to me when I finally collapsed.

My collapse occurred during one of those infrequent times Pam and I were in the canoe rather than carrying it. We had been paddling a good five minutes when we came upon what I knew all at once had to be my last deadfall. Propping myself up in the boat, looking at the enormous tangle of the dead tree in front of us, and the wetness and steepness of the banks beside us, I suddenly couldn't lift my arms or legs. I could no longer negotiate about what we were to do next. I needed to sleep so badly that I felt drugged or drunk, and I didn't care where I did it, provided I slept right where I was.

"Pam," I spoke into her back desperately, "I have to stop right now; I've got to lie down."

"We can't stop now," she answered without turning around. "It's almost dark. We don't want to get stuck here with the canoe, do we? We don't want to have to leave the boat." She glanced over her shoulder, saw me, and frowned. She had finally let herself acknowledge that perhaps we were about to find ourselves in a very bad place.

By this time, I was beyond caring. I knew, however, that she was indeed right about the darkness. By now it was coming in so fast that the outlines of the trees above us and even the sight of the banks next to us were fading before our eyes. The light was slipping away from us without any stopping as quickly as consciousness at the hands of an anesthesiologist before surgery. The loss of light should have been frightening, but I was way past feeling it.

"I don't care about the boat," I said. "We're going to have to abandon it." This was not just my tiredness speaking: inexperienced at this sort of thing as I was, I was the only one of us still, I think, who had the faintest idea how far we actually were from the place down the river where our car was parked.

Since the boat was mine, Pam was not about to humor me on the matter of leaving the canoe. I, after all, would later be the one of us without it. Her own beautiful but fragile canoe, which she had built with her own hands from delicate strips of wood, was back home in Atlanta, hanging safely from the ceiling of her garage.

"We can't possibly keep on with the boat," I went on, fighting for my sleep. "Even if I didn't feel like I do, Pam, how could you and I carry it in the dark through all this stuff? We wouldn't be able to do it, even if Jeff were able to help us."

Involuntarily, both of us glanced up at the bank over our heads to look for Jeff. Not having noticed that we had stopped, or at least unable to join the conversation, he had not quit walking when we stopped in the water. Using his canoe paddle as a combination crutch and cane, big chin in the air, he was still very slowly pushing himself along the tangled, sodden ground. Together, we watched his stiff back for a moment before Pam called out to him.

"Jeff," she shouted. With his energy concentrated on his knee, he didn't hear her. Pam climbed out of the canoe, stood in the water beside the giant root ball of the toppled tree before us and yelled into her cupped hands two or three more times.

"Jeff, Jeff!"

This time he heard her and turned around. "What?" he called back dully. One word was all he could squeeze out; it was without expression.

"We've got to take a rest," Pam answered.

Crazed as I was, I was not too exhausted to be shamed and embarrassed by my insistence that we stop, nor was I too tired to appreciate the fact that Pam had just said, "We need a rest," and not, "I can't get Roberta to keep going." She wasn't about to lay the responsibility for what could prove to be a dangerous rest on my shoulders, though that is certainly where it belonged. With a flood of love for Pam that was itself a grace, I remembered a story about one of my good teachers of the Egyptian desert that was recounted in the Sayings of the Fathers:

> One day when Abba John was going up to Scetis with some other brothers, their guide lost his way for it was night-time. So the brothers said to Abba John, "What shall we do, Abba, in order not to die wandering about, for the brother has lost the way?" The old man said to them, "If we speak to him, he will be filled with grief and shame. But look here, I will pretend to be ill and say I cannot walk any more; then we can stay here till the dawn." This he did. The others said, "We will not go on either, but we will stay with you." They sat there until the dawn, and in this way they did not upset the brother.[1]

Even in my stubborn exhaustion Pam's refusal to blame me for slowing us down and putting us in danger overwhelmed me with such gratitude it could have made me weep.

Wounded Jeff, I suspect, was hardly thinking about or feeling this sort of thing, however. Up on the bank, he was leaning hard on his paddle; he pivoted himself around on his good leg and started slowly back toward us without a further answer to Pam's call.

I stuck my own paddle in the water beside where I sat in the boat and pulled myself up, I am not proud to say,

---

1. John the Dwarf, 17, *The Sayings of the Desert Fathers*, trans. Benedicta Ward (Oxford: Mowbray, 1975), p. 89.

whimpering a little as the gritty weight of my wet sweat-pants pulled at my waist. As night had come on, my pants had become cold against my legs as well as wet and heavy.

Pam took me by the arm and helped me out, patting and fussing over me at the same time. She propped me up against the root ball of the tree in the water, then bent back over the boat. "Let's make sure to get your stuff out of the canoe," she said. "We don't want to leave any-thing."

I didn't care whether I left anything or not. "I have to lie down," I answered, urgently. By now, getting prone was a need as strong and compelling as the need to vomit.

"Just go on up the bank, then," she said, kindly; "I'll take care of things here."

I slipped and scrambled on my hands and knees and pulled myself up the muddy bank. I noticed at a distance that the skin on my hands stung and all my joints hurt. I stood on the mushy ground a minute without moving; I'd used the little remaining energy I'd had dragging myself through the mud from the river.

Then Jeff was back. He and Pam, who had climbed up behind me, immediately huddled to decide between them what we should do. There was no point in trying to include me in the conversation; I was uninterested.

"I have to go to sleep," I said to them once more. "I need to sleep right now."

Worried, Pam turned around to answer. "But there's nothing for you to lie down on," she said. "The ground is soaking wet."

"I don't care how wet it is," I replied. "I'm lying

down." As best as I remember, I took off my dirty rain-coat and spread it over the thick layer of utterly soggy leaves at my feet and collapsed on it; as I stretched out on it the ground squished and gave beneath me. I closed my eyes. What difference did it make whether I chose one spot rather than another? With everything as soaked as it was, I couldn't have found a better place, anyway, even if it had been possible to see to look for one, which by now it wouldn't have been.

In less than a minute I was almost entirely asleep. The two of them had quit whispering. I could hear them making some other sounds I had no interest in identify-ing. There was a rustling, crackling noise I didn't recog-nize. Then Pam lay down beside me, and Jeff beside Pam—I could tell from a sudden sound of two people breathing close to my ear—then a piece of slick foil the thickness and consistency of plastic wrap floated down over us.

"Emergency space blanket," Pam said, triumphantly. She loves her camping equipment. Tonight, this was the only piece she had with her, and she was proud to have remembered it.

She put her arms around me from the back and cud-dled up on the spongy ground to warm and comfort me. "I love you," she said in her beautiful voice.

Suddenly full of an unexpected happiness, which poured out of a gift of gratitude for the very being of my friend, I answered her, "I love you, too."

These were our last words before I fell asleep like someone falling down a well and into the arms of God.

I have not always known Pam or loved her. I met her

first ten years ago at a summer professional conference in Oxford we were both attending. I had never seen her before that day when she came up to me in the Sommerville quad at teatime to tell me that she was interested in teaching in our seminary. She told me she was thirty-five or so, ten years younger than I, and still writing her dissertation on the feminization of poverty. She had two children by a former marriage, and she wanted me to tell her what it might be like for her if she were to come to Atlanta.

I was hardly able to answer. Being the introvert I am, I was already thoroughly worn out from my duties, listening and responding to the other members of the conference over the previous week or so. I was also a bit dazed from the emotional exertion of keeping my temporal bearings since I was back in Oxford where I had done my graduate work in another life more than twenty years earlier. I remember taking in Pam's slightly pushy energy, her shiny black hair, her dark brown eyes and compact body with dismay. I gave her some sort of offputting reply, a bit rude, it seemed, from my perspective, not because I meant to be rude, but because I could hardly help it.

She was hired at our school the next year, I believe, if not the one after that, with no thanks to me. I was on sabbatical and not in any way a part of the hiring. I had very few feelings about her coming, except that I was glad to have another woman on the faculty. Once she was there, those first few semesters we hardly ever saw each other. Richard and I were struggling not to go under as we tried to rear a quiet child and a volatile adolescent, and I was trying to find a way to write that suited me. Pam was recently remarried and attempting to adjust to life with a man who had left a good job in Chicago to come down with her. The adjustment was made harder, as she would tell me on the infrequent occasions when I saw her, by the fact that she and her new husband were coping with one disaster after another in the lemon of a house they had bought in a distant suburb. All in all, Pam and I were in very different places in our lives; it was also clear to me that we were also of very different temperaments and interests.

It was really not until the next Oxford conference, five years later, that I began to get to know her. I had come over to Oxford for another, unrelated church meeting a few days prior to the conference. The event had gone well enough from an objective standpoint; the five other participants seemed pleased with our work. For a number of reasons, however (including the fact that I was the only woman in what was an intensely male group who had no interest in conversation with me), it had taken every emotional, intellectual, and spiritual resource I had just to get through it. I never really have trouble doing my work in meetings such as this; rather, I collapse in a heap of unbearable anxiety and self-recrimination afterward. It was certainly the case this time. By the last day of the meeting, I was so anxious and demoralized, I could hardly think of what to do with myself.

Fortunately, I remembereded that Pam and Rebecca, another woman on our faculty with whom we were both friends, had come over early before the Oxford conference to rent a hotel room in London for two nights, and before

I left they had invited me to join them. I wasn't sure that I was up to much more human company, but I recalled their invitation, and by some miracle of grace I was able to dig out from my purse the name of the place where they were staying. By a second miracle, I managed immediately to get Pam and Rebecca on the phone and arranged to meet them that afternoon at their room in the hotel.

That trip to London was the first occasion on which I really spent time with Pam. I can't say that I got to know her then, but in those two days I did find out something of her capacity for fun, her love of adventure, and her ability to enjoy herself, all of which were characteristics in myself in those particular days that were painfully in need of cultivating. It was as much of a relief to be with her and Rebecca as it is to lie down in a good bed when I'm tired. Oddly, apart from a trip to the British Museum, my favorite place in the whole of London, I don't remember much concretely of what the three of us did or where we went.

I remember our time as wonderful. We ate a lot of Indian food, I think, comfort food for me from my Oxford days in the sixties, and I vaguely recall leaning out the hotel window to look into the tops of the trees and breathe in the old familiar smell of black exhaust from the red double-decker buses on the road outside our room. There were dazzling patches of red and yellow flowers against the grass in the park outside the hotel, sunlight on the Serpentine, shiny black wrought-iron railings marking off the entrances to basement flats around the British Museum, and the long yellow tile walls of the Underground.

In Oxford once more, I was back in big conference mode. I heard Pam respond brilliantly, I thought, to a major address one afternoon toward the end of our two weeks, but apart from that, I saw little of her until the long flight home, which we had discovered in London we were to share. We met on the last day and took the train to Heathrow where we exchanged our tickets so that we could travel together.

Several hours later, we found ourselves side by side in two miserable middle seats of the plane, squished so tightly between the other passengers we could hardly move. Still, this was our big chance. We were able to lean back on our lumpy jackets with our feet on our luggage, and talk with each other at last of our former and present lives, our children, our husbands, our work, and our varying commitments, as well as of our pleasures, our sorrows, and our stresses. Though I was fast discovering how different Pam and I really were—she an outspoken midwestern extrovert, I a southern, much more indirect introvert; she with her energies focused on public issues and the transformation of church and society, and I with a deep distrust of both; she with a self-confidence in the goodness of her own motives and abilities, and I with a painful number of doubts about my own—I found that I liked Pam enormously. There was nothing of cosmic significance to my liking. We simply giggled and told secrets like teenagers, cried together, shared food stories and tales of the women in our families until our plane touched down nine hours later in Georgia.

While I wondered about Pam frequently, life was too busy for both of us to see each other much that fall after we returned. I was surprised when she called at the beginning of November to suggest that she and I have an overnight camping trip in the Okefenokee Swamp the first weekend in December. Because I already travel so much and prefer not to be away from Richard when I don't have to be, ordinarily I wouldn't have accepted. I had never recovered from the summer, however, and the preceding months of teaching and writing had worn me down more than usual. I had not one bit of experience with the kind of primitive camping we would have to do (would I be eaten by an alligator, I wondered?), and hardly anything good could be expected of the winter weather. Still, the idea of all that water, silence, and lack of human obligation appealed mightily.

We took off after school on a Friday a month later. Our van loaded down according to Pam's directions, with a canoe, paddles, life jackets, a tent, small lantern and stove, matches, sleeping bags, sleeping pads, clean underwear and socks, food supplies, drinking water, rain gear, and books, our supplies did not resemble in any respect those we were to carry later to the Flint River.

Though it rained the whole of the five hours or so we were driving, I felt myself relaxing in the van for the first time in months. Pam and I ate corn chips, talked a little about nothing particularly important, and listened to a mystery on tape we'd rented along the way. It was nearly dark when we reached the edge of the swamp which was our destination. We drove around a while through brown fields, past unpainted houses with barking dogs, across a railroad track until we found the deserted, grassy place we would come back to in order to enter the swamp the next morning. After that, we located a motel, where I suffered the indignity of being given a senior citizen's discount, ate a big supper in the motel restaurant, and went to bed.

We got up the next morning, ate again, and drove in a continuing light rain to our put-in point, a spot so deserted that the only sign of human presence in it was a rustic box with a book inside it in which to sign our names so that the park rangers would know to look for our bodies after a few days if we didn't come back out. We heaved the canoe off the van and put it in the water, loaded it with our supplies, and locked the van. Then we started out, following the colored trail markers spaced at long intervals on trees or inconspicuous guideposts ahead of us.

We were both excited to be in that exotic place. In spite of the rain and the cold, we were not uncomfortable. Both of us were clothed in rain gear and warm clothes from head to toe. Because there was no current and we had all day to get where we were going, paddling was easy. We saw another boat at a distance a half hour or so into the trip, but no other human beings after that.

We began our trip on black, open water, surrounded by trees and small islands. Only an hour or so later the landscape had changed entirely. Now we found ourselves paddling in silence on a narrow, very shallow stream that cut through smooth, marshy fields of thick, pale green grasses that grew in every direction as far as we could see.

It seemed to me that we were at the end of the world, or rather, at its beginning before the creation of trees as well as of human beings, and, though I wouldn't have admitted it to Pam, it was frightening as well as exhilarating. There were no visible alligators, but there were a lot of turtles and birds of every kind, some we recognized and some we didn't. Unnaturally white snowy egrets sunk their legs in pools of standing water and flew over us in flocks. We saw blue herons, little brown water birds, hawks, and larger birds we would have liked to believe were eagles, though they were probably vultures seen at a distance. In fact, there were more vultures than any other kind of bird we saw, big vultures that followed along behind us, waiting, no doubt, for one of us to make a mistake, fall overboard, and be attacked by a hibernating alligator.

We got to the covered platform in the water where we were to pitch our tent much earlier than we expected. We tethered the boat, jumped onto the small dock, then unloaded and set up our tent within sight of a large bare tree full of horribly interested vultures. Even now, Pam and I don't agree on how many vultures there actually were; I think it was twenty; she, about two. Whatever their number, however, a particularly large one scared us half to death later in the afternoon when it flew invisibly over us and landed with a heavy crash on the tin roof immediately above our heads.

Apart from this particular fright, however, the rest of the day was deeply peaceful. The ground around the platform was too marshy to hike on, so there was nothing to do but stay where we were. We made hot chocolate over our toy stove, had a nap in the tent, still dressed in our rain clothes, then crawled back out about four o'clock to make tuna-rice casserole and camping cake. By now, at ease with each other, we felt no need to say much of anything. Darkness fell as we were cleaning up; in spite of the cold and rain, it was a soft darkness in which to rest in God.

We went to bed in our pup tent, each in two sleeping bags. We read for a while by the light of our small electric lantern, and went soundly to sleep at seven o'clock. The next morning, after a breakfast of coffee and oatmeal fortified with nuts and raisins, we took down our camp, paddled uneventfully back to the van, and drove to Atlanta to give exams at school and to prepare for Christmas.

It was two months, perhaps, before I really saw Pam again. I knew she was having an increasingly hard time at home and that she was coping with her troubles by building herself a complicated, beautiful canoe out of thin strips of wood in her garage. She invited me out several times to view her project, but I was never able to go.

One day in the early spring, she called me to tell me she wanted to talk. When we got together over coffee the next afternoon, she told me her marriage was over; she knew she could count on me for emotional support. She needed to move out of the house, she said, but she had to have a place to stay for a little while as she decided where and how she would live. Her daughters were both in college; she only had to have a bed for herself. Richard and I had a tiny guest room off the kitchen. She wouldn't be eating with us. Would we mind if she stayed with us just for a bit?

I was a little taken aback—after all, it hadn't been that long since Ben had moved out, and Richard and I were still getting used to that—but I went home and talked it over with Richard. Both of us remembered only too well from our former lives what it had been like to be in a situation comparable to hers. We decided we needed to help, especially since I was beginning to have something of a sense of how sociable Pam really was, and how hard it would be for her to be completely by herself at such a time.

What began as a favor to Pam immediately became a pleasure. I might say that Pam worked hard at being a considerate guest, except that I never actually felt her to be working at it. Most days, she was up early and gone to the gym before we were even out of bed. We rarely saw her before the middle of the evening when she would come in, sometimes sad with the knowledge of the way in which her hopes had slipped out from under her, but more often laughing with a happy energy she was determined would carry her into another and better place in her life. The whole time she was with us, I found that there was something significantly healing in her company.

The year I turned fifty had been a kind of transition year for me. My beloved aunt had died the summer before, and in that spring my father also died. I'd been gone an uncomfortably long time to Singapore and Australia over the summer without Richard. In September my mother had very serious heart surgery that almost killed her. Excruciatingly aware of my losses—accomplished, impending, and imaginary—as well as of my own mortality, that year I made a number of decisions both about my work and about life as I wanted to lead the rest of it. One of these decisions was to take up playing the flute again after having set it aside for thirty-two years.

I speak of it now as a decision, but that is not strictly accurate; taking up the flute again was more a compulsion than a choice. Where it came from, I hardly know. I had passionately loved my flute as an adolescent, but my father's perfectionism ("What point is there in playing an instrument if you are not going to be a professional?") added to my own had defeated me completely. As a child and a teenager, I had never been able to believe that I was capable of learning anything that mattered, much less something as beautiful and shining as a flute, and so I had never practiced. What good would it have done if I had? I played in the school band and orchestra, nevertheless, and I loved it. It was logical that I sell my flute as part of my attempt to stop being who I was and claim a new identity for myself when I married at eighteen.

For whatever reason, however, in my fiftieth year, I could no longer live with the consequences of such a stupid decision. The marriage had ended long ago; now the flute was suddenly necessary to me again. On the Friday closest to my birthday I went out by myself and bought a new student instrument, without talking it over with anyone. I brought it home and began to play it immediately. Though I had long since lost the muscles for it, miraculously I could still remember its fingerings.

I played my new flute all that weekend till Richard's ears rung and my mouth and cheeks refused to move. It gave me the most intense happiness to play. It was like falling in love; it was like the re-establishment of a friendship from childhood once accidentally broken; it was like a dream of flying over mountains in the sun. How can I say it? It was finding a part of myself that had been lost, and it was discovering a part of God.

During that whole first year when my flute was my prayer, as I played, the Holy Spirit seemed to hover in the sounds of it like God above the primeval waters. Soon, I was taking lessons from a real teacher again, and, unlike in high school, this time I practiced. Still, I found that I was easily demoralized in the old ways of childhood by my inability to get right what I was attempting as quickly as I thought I should. Then, again, I would frequently find myself hearing my own playing like a critical and hostile stranger listening to an incompetent child, and all of a sudden I would fall into a crushing sense of shame, unworthiness, and darkness from which I could not extricate myself.

It was about a year after I had begun again on my flute, when I was wrestling with some of the worst of this, that Pam came to stay. Pam, who often was in the house in the evenings when I was practicing, had no sense of the intensity of my feelings around my flute, my highs and lows, my globalizing despairings and my cosmic joys. She was interested neither in how well or how badly I played. It wasn't that she was insensitive. Rather, she was excited by the idea of a middle-aged woman like me taking up, or taking up again, a musical instrument because she wanted to. To Pam, that was wonderful fun.

Within a few days of coming to our house, she sent word to her brother for her grandmother's violin, which she had played for a short time in the fifth grade. Soon she was standing in the middle of our exercise room at ten o'clock at night, her instrument tucked under her chin on a red bandanna, playing simple hymn tunes with her characteristic enthusiasm.

Pam was so funny and dear with respect to her music, and so good for me. Her own approach was cheerfully extroverted, the very opposite of my own introverted, soul-searching way of being. When it came to music, she had nothing of the compulsive about her, no interest in formal lessons. She certainly never considered failure to get what she was playing right to be a matter for shame. A mistake was never more than a mistake. For her, it was not a cause for despair, no visible and outward sign of an invisible and inward unworthiness. She was so proud of herself that first week as she stood on the rose-colored rug in the exercise room screeching out "Joy to the World" in dirge time, missing notes and playing out of tune so badly it made my teeth hurt.

She would come to the end of whatever piece she was playing and look at me, her face glowing with triumph and pleasure. "What do you think of that?" she would ask. "Pretty good, huh?"

"It was great, Pam," I would reply, dazed and dazzled by the whole thing.

I was not surprised when within less than a week Pam decided that she and I needed to begin to play duets in the evenings. Though Richard was generally at his computer when she came back to our house at ten or so, I was nearly always reading in bed, often even asleep. Still, she would call out a drawn-out "hell-*ooo*" as she came through the kitchen door. A few minutes later I would hear the sounds of things being dropped on the floor, walking in the living room, and tooth-brushing in the bathroom, then a "snap, snap" from the exercise room across the hall from our bedroom as she opened her black violin case.

At this point, I would lie down flat, if I were not prone already, pull the covers up over my ears and try to look asleep. I don't think my ploy worked a single time. Sneaking glances between closed eyelids, I'd watch Pam walk energetically into our bedroom, grinning with excitement, her violin in one hand and her bow in the other.

"Okay, Bobbie," she'd say to me (she was the only one who could get away with calling me by my old baby name). "Time to get up and get out the flute." While Richard laughed bemusedly at us from his spot by the computer, she'd wait a moment or two to see if I were about to wiggle under the blankets or otherwise give away the fact that I was still awake. Then she would add enticingly, "Don't you want to play 'The Three Ds'?" "The Three Ds" is what she called my favorite song in our hymnbook whose first three notes happen to be "D." Actually, this is an Advent song, known more commonly as "People, Look East."

"Pam, I can't get up," I would moan, whining as I buried myself deeper into the blankets. "I had a really long day."

Then, Pam would rock back and forth on the balls of her feet and begin playing scales, excruciatingly out of tune.

"Sure, you can get up," she'd say, grinning some more. "How can you resist me?"

And I don't think I did resist, finally, not a single time. Physically, getting up to play with her was like getting up in the middle of the night when the children were babies, but it was good, too, to be with Pam and see the innocence and thoroughness of her pleasure. We would squeak out one hymn after another, exchanging alto and soprano when she thought she could manage. For her, I could set aside my pressing shame around my need to play well.

When I could hardly stand up any longer, I would tell her that I had to quit and she would be satisfied. Generally we ended on a few verses of "Shall We Gather at the River?" which was a favorite for both of us, then she would hug me and go off to her room, still humming to herself, while I climbed back in bed and this time truly went to sleep.

It was an odd interlude in the lives of Pam and me, wonderfully full of God in many ways. I was sorry when she moved out and into her own apartment, and Richard was, too. I saw her much less frequently after that. She certainly continued to be a part of our family life. She still took a great interest in Ben, who was off at college in Indiana. Grace and Dugan, our son-in-law, asked her to perform their wedding ceremony the next year after the Flint River. The summer after that when Richard and I were both out of town and Grace had unexpected surgery, Pam went with her and stayed with her. Through all this time when Pam herself was feeling low or suffering from too much chaos, she would come back to our house to be fed a good meal, "sleep in her own bed," and be pampered by us.

Two years or more after what I believed would be our fatal adventure together, and Richard's counseling practice had begun to entail his regular absence from home during three weeknights, Pam and I developed a habit of eating leftovers together on Thursday evenings, sometimes in her house and sometimes in mine. We would sink comfortably into each other's company, make a little terrible music on the flute and violin when Pam was in the mood, and play double-jump killer Chinese checkers for a while; then two hours later, each of us would return much refreshed to our work as well as to all the other parts of our lives that commanded our attention, our energies, and our love.

But the thought of those evenings brings me back now to the place where I lay down on the soaked ground beside the Flint River and my later puzzlings in prayer over the meaning of the things that happened there that night, of God, and friendship and what it means to be a human being in God's world. How elusive and difficult to articulate are the insights that have come to me, a mixture as they are, seen darkly through a glass of my own reason and experience, of words spoken to me by teachers dead for centuries, of scripture, of present and past loves, of my husband, my parents, my aunts, my children, my students, even my cat. I find none of this easy to put into words, and yet, because it has come to me in the form of gifts, and is still coming as gifts, gratitude compels me, almost against my inclinations, to try.

And, here, in the peculiar reality of the gratitude I felt

back there beside the Flint River, drenched as I was and stretched out on a thick layer of wet leaves, expecting to die soon—here is where I would begin. First, I must say that I still can't quite make sense of the force and complexity of this gratitude, or even specify precisely to whom it was directed. I know it had a lot to do, however, with an odd sense of coming out from under judgment.

The oldest child of two young, perfectionistic parents who were both convinced that I could do very little right and that my every action at any given minute was about to reflect badly upon them, I grew up with a sense of living under a continual negative human judgment rendered or about to be rendered against me. Regular trips during summer revival to my mother's childhood country Baptist church easily convinced me that God expected far more of me than my parents and was even angrier and more disappointed than they over who I was. To make matters worse, once having left my childhood home, I spent the years between eighteen and thirty-five in an excruciatingly anxious marriage in which I could not please my husband. I was bitterly blamed by him for everything in the universe that made him unhappy, including not only forgetting to bring home all the items on the grocery list, but also bad weather and his father's death.

By the time of this incident on the Flint River, I had not lived with the helpless depression which was my response to the disappointed angry expectations of my nearest and dearest for a very long time. Not only had I begun long ago through my prayer to learn how differently God really saw me than I had always feared; I had also left my first husband nearly twenty years earlier, and both of my parents had eased up on themselves, me, and their other children considerably as they grew older. Even more important, by now I had been married for sixteen years to Richard, whose intelligent, uncritical, and gentle love for me surrounded and sustained me day to day.

Still, in situations of extreme stress, we often find ourselves turning back to the surviving remnants of our old ways of feeling, seeing, and being. That night, this was what happened to me. As night fell, my very body began to brace itself against the familiar expectations of anger and blame. When Pam responded to my panicky demand that I lie down with cheerful calmness and love and without explosive touchiness or blaming, I was so grateful I could taste it in my mouth and feel it in my fingers as a sensation of physical well-being. It was an experience of human love, but it was also an overwhelming experience of God.

But what do I mean that it was an experience of God? It was not God who exhibited this patience. It was Pam, and Pam was certainly herself that night, completely herself, no more or less than a good and in most ways an ordinary woman with whom I had come home from England and camped in the Okefenokee, and above all, with whom I had enjoyed playing dreadful duets in my own exercise room.

But listen to what lies behind this saying from the ancient Egyptian desert, both about God and about human beings who become like God:

> They said of Abba Macarius the Great that he became, as
> it is written, a god upon earth, because, just as God pro-
> tects the world, so Abba Macarius would cover the faults
> which he saw, as though he did not see them; and those
> which he heard, as though he did not hear them.[2]

For me, in that hard time, Pam was not only a good
friend and a woman like myself. That night she was also
Abba Macarius, become like God—God who "protects
the world," "covering the faults which [she] saw as
though [she] did not see them."

As the Abbas and Ammas who, by their nonjudgmen-
tal sympathy, lifted the most dreadful burdens of blame
and self-recrimination from the shoulders of those whose
paths they crossed, Pam's love carved out for me a space
in the wilderness in which it was safe to breathe and
accept in trust of God's good love, what I thought was
my own impending death.

The space carved out for me, of course, was God's
space, and Pam's presence not only her own but also
God's. How easily and lightly I had talked before about
the importance of being God to each other! I am not so
sure I had ever realized with such clarity, however, how
literally this language speaks. Now I know it: there are
times, not when human beings are changed into some
superhuman goodness or nobility, but when we are most
ourselves, as Pam was then, when to speak of becoming
"God to each other" is peculiarly accurate.

Or, to try to say the same thing from the other end:
Through the generous and loving goodness of God, it

2. Macarius the Great 32, p. 134.

seems that it sometimes happens, especially in times of need, that one of us, an ordinary human being who never ceases to be the tattered image of God she or he has always been, becomes completely transparent to God for someone else so that for a little while, the one in need can see God truly through that human being. For me that night Pam was transparent in this way. Flawed like the rest of us, she did not cease to be herself. Rather, it was her same lack of anxiety over wrong notes played on the violin or flute in our common music that was the vehicle of her gift of God on the Flint River. Indeed, it was through a grasping of the irrelevance of my weakness to her love of me that I was able to come that night to a sure knowledge of the equally uncritical and most improbable love of God who, Julian of Norwich tells us, even in our weakness, failures and sin,

> never allows us to be alone, but constantly [God] is with us, and tenderly [God] excuses us, and always protects us from blame [in God's sight].[3]

Thus were laid to rest in me the last remnants of the thought that God would meet me at my death only to search out my sins to blame and punish me.

How radical to think that God should not blame, but protect us from such blame, and yet, as I learned from what was said of Abba Macarius, from Julian, and from Pam who showed it to me that night on the Flint River, it is true! How full of gratitude I am to all of them, and to

3. Long Text, chapter eighty, p. 336.

God most of all who gives the gratitude that allows us to receive God's other gifts!

But more on gratitude later; let me return now to my original story, to the place next to Pam where I was, on the ground by the Flint River. Believe me; I didn't lie there long. Sometime very soon after I lay down and was covered with her so-called space blanket, Pam shook me gently to wake me.

"Roberta, we have to go on," she said. "Jeff is only wearing a T-shirt and shorts. His knee is beginning to freeze up and the temperature is dropping fast. We really won't ever get him out of here unless we keep walking."

Awake at once, I reached for my paddle and pulled myself up, noticing as I did so that, though I was wet to the skin from the water that had condensed on the metal blanket, I felt amazingly much better than I had the few minutes before.

I was worried about Jeff, whom I had no more intention of abandoning than Pam had of abandoning me, no matter how tired I might become.

At this point, Pam interrupted my thoughts. "Time to eat," she said. She patted down the length of my arm and found my hand, into which she put half of one of the energy bars which she had got out of my pack while I was still asleep. To Jeff, who was the size of both of us together, she gave the other one. We split the rest of the pretzels and the red licorice among the three of us, then washed down our meal with precious mouthfuls of water from our jug.

By this time we were in total darkness.

Chapter 3

Darkness

I looked to where the sky should have been in hopes of a hint that a moon was up there somewhere waiting to appear at the proper time to help us find a path through the wilderness to home. There was nothing to see, no sliver of brightness, no faint glow, no dark and darker, no hint of the silhouette of a tree or a vine against a backdrop of a not-quite-so-black horizon. As the rain of the preceding four days had left behind the thick blanket of soaked leaves beneath our feet, it seemed to me that it had also so saturated the air through which we were to walk that it had become impenetrable to light.

I wasn't actually afraid. The sky had disappeared, it is true, and the ground along with it, but I myself was most certainly still there; and if this were the case, I knew my own body in some way would have to be reassuringly visible, no matter how faint. I squinted my eyes and looked down in vain through the solid air as I searched for my feet. There were no feet to be seen.

I drew in a shaky breath. I raised my hands to my face, first the left and then the right, as though one were more likely to appear than the other. Again, there was nothing to see—no muddy palms, no gritty fingers, not so much as the hint of a scratched wrist or a dirty sleeve. We were in darkness the likes of which I had experienced only in childhood dreams.

It was like being without light in a cave under the earth, like being shut up in a small, close closet. There was nothing to distinguish far from near, up from down, even me from not me. If I couldn't see it did I still have a body? Suddenly, it came to me that the darkness in which I found myself might well be the darkness of death. Was I, in fact, dead? Panic rising, I stamped my feet and blew out a breath. I reached up and slapped my chilled jaws one at a time with a muddy hand. My face stung from the slaps and my hand hurt from the embedded grit and cuts. The pain of it filled me with relief. The rest of the world had disappeared; I might actually be dead. But I hurt, and hurting told me that my body, at least, was still joined to the rest of me, was still mine.

With this discovery the darkness around me began to come to life with the beneficent sound of human movement. I couldn't hear Jeff, but Pam I could hear, blessedly creaking, rustling, and making zipping noises somewhere in front of me, and I was filled with gratitude for the sounds she made.

Pam. In a moment she called out to me in her beautiful Minnesota voice that always rings in my ears like singing. "Bobbie?" she said. "Where are you?"

Relief washed through me again as I heard her call me by this name. It pushed the heaviness of the darkness away from my face and off my chest and told me emphatically that I was alive and not, in fact, alone in the universe, cut off from the rest of the human race.

I cleared my throat, slapped myself on the chest a time or two and answered her in my own boring, flat Kentucky accent. "Pammy, is that you?"

"It's Pammy, all right," she said. Through the thick air I could hear her laughing. "Who did you think I might be?"

Bobbie and Pammy. How good it was to hear and speak these silly names of ours! They were a kind of joke between us that had arisen on our trip to London when we were first getting to know each other. "Bobbie" was my baby name, but I had allowed nobody to use it after I became a flat-chested, scrawny twelve-year-old who'd been sensitive about being mistaken for a boy. "Pammy" was the equally hated name Pam's family had called her as a child.

The first night I was in London, Pam and I had confessed these names to each other and to Rebecca, our third friend with us. Rebecca had been called "Becky" as a little girl, and she had despised her nickname as much as we had our own. After we had put on our pajamas and turned out the lights in our white hotel room, the three of us had lain in our narrow beds and giggled, remembering our innocent early adolescent longings to be adult and sophisticated. Then we had pretended to be the three nice, docile little girls our poor parents had wanted us to be—three children out on the kind of adventure we read about in the goody-goody storybooks we'd each been given. Bobbie and Pammy: the two of us had privately continued to use these names for each other ever since, at least whenever we got out our flute and violin or otherwise were having fun rather than doing serious work.

At any rate, I knew very well that though I might die that night—and I certainly still believed that I would—the Pam who called me "Bobbie" was not going to leave me alone in the darkness if she could help it. I straightened my back and began to try to think. "What are we going to do?" I asked, by now much bucked up and prepared to walk, whatever my expectation of the outcome. "I can't see a thing."

"Well," Pam answered, "the three of us are going to have to walk along the bank and try to follow the river. It's the only way we'll get out." Her voice faded as though she were facing away from me. "I think I can see an animal trail in front of me."

Seeing nothing myself, I was baffled over how this could be, but she insisted that the bank was to her, in fact, faintly visible. Behind me Jeff made a few grunting sounds of assent.

"But how will we be able to walk?" I still couldn't imagine it. "You may be able to find a trail, but I can't see enough to follow you. In fact, I can't see anything. And what about Jeff?"

Again, Jeff grunted somewhere to my back, then spoke up gruffly. "Listen, I've got to move," he said. His voice sounded squeezed up through his chest and out through his teeth. "Pam can go in front; Roberta can walk behind and grab the back of her coat, and I'll come behind her." His voice stopped for a moment, then it resumed. "I think I can see a little bit," he said. "I don't have to hold on to anything besides my paddle."

"Okay," I answered. "I don't know what else we can do," I said, and I didn't. I wanted to ask him how his knee was feeling, but I knew that he was managing the pain of it by turning his attention away from it by going into a distant part of himself into which he did not wish to be followed.

I left him alone, and inched up slowly until I ran into Pam's back, then picked up the hem of her jacket. "I'm here," I said.

When it comes to the outdoors, Pam loves the difficult, even the dangerous. I suspect they make her feel strong and resourceful, which she is. So far on our trip she had shown no sign of fear or anxiety even when we had had to abandon the canoe, and she didn't show them now. "Have you got your paddle?" she asked me cheerfully. I could hear her whacking the bushes and ground in front of her with energy.

"Yup," I replied, leaning my weight on the wooden handle thankfully. "I've got it right here."

"If you stick your paddle out in front of you, you can guide yourself with it," she said. "You ought to be able to use it to feel for holes and trees in your path."

"I know," I answered. I'd caught myself with my bent-wood paddle two or three times already in the last five minutes as I'd begun to trip over a root or fall into a hole.

There was nothing else to say. Pam in front, we began to shuffle our way through the wet underbrush and trees. Now, I was concentrating so hard on walking that the thought of death was almost peripheral to my consciousness.

Though she was moving very slowly, Pam did seem to

be able to see a little. Within a few minutes it was apparent that she could go much faster than I, stumbling along as I was, and faster still than the wounded Jeff, whom I could hear breathing hard at my back.

I was too proud to complain or ask for quarter. Fortunately, Jeff was not. "Pam," he said at last behind me, "what are you trying to do? There is no way we can keep up with you if you keep on like this."

"Really?" asked Pam, surprised. "I'm sorry." She slowed down at once, and soon we were picking our way along at such a crawl that I supposed we were hardly moving at all.

Having established our pace, we went on like this for hours, though I couldn't say for how many since none of us could see the faces on our watches. It was certainly long enough for me to have done a lot of falling down. I must have stepped in thirty-five holes or more those first few hours in the dark. Each time I would stick my paddle in the underbrush before me, believing myself to be on solid ground. The next thing I knew, I would have stepped off into nothing, slipping hard on my rear end into a marshy dip or even a real hole where tree roots once had been.

Pam, who was trying to keep her eye on the track, ignored my falling, but Jeff admired my ability to leap right back up again whenever I fell. I never told him that my leaping was hardly motivated by courage or good character. True, I certainly had no intention of lying on the ground, whimpering in self-pity. My real motivation, however, was a phobic fear of snakes: every time I reached out to find the invisible tree into which I was already walking I imagined that I was about to put my hand down on a cold, thick brown snake draped sullenly over some slimy branch. Was I afraid of snakebite from water moccasin or copperhead, which I knew very well lived in abundance along the river? I was indeed, but you must understand that it was contact with the snakes themselves I feared even more than their poison. This was the real reason I jumped back up as soon as I fell. Death didn't seem so bad; still, I had inherited the curse of Eve; it was simply coming in contact with a snake that horrified me.

Of course, even then I never pretended that my fear of snakes was entirely realistic. Certainly, there were many people later—people without sense who weren't even there that night—who insisted that the multitude of those reptiles that coiled along the riverbanks would surely have been hibernating. I knew very well that even if they weren't peacefully asleep in their dens, those snakes could have heard us clumping through the woods in plenty of time to slither off and hide.

Whether or not I was realistic in my fear of snakes, however, I was not so unrealistic with respect to the gun-shots that had exploded periodically but regularly from the time we had set off at noon until far into the night. Richard had warned us before we'd set out that this was the opening weekend for deer season, and there would probably be hunters afoot. There was something eerie and terrible about walking hour after hour in the pitch dark-ness with no visible sign of human habitation, no house or barn or even field (though we had caught sight of a pas-ture around four o'clock the preceding afternoon) while we heard those guns. The fact is that another real danger hid in the darkness in addition to that of hypothermia, thirst, or accidental injury. The anonymous guns were real.

Still, there is darkness, and then there is darkness: certainly even expecting to die, what I faced that night on the Flint River was nothing compared to my childhood fear of the dark. Certainly, I was always afraid of the dark, always afraid of what it did to me and what might come to me in it. "If I should die before I wake I pray the Lord my soul to take" was hardly a prayer of comfort. I was afraid of sleep, for frequently I had almost hallucinatory dreams that I had accidentally been taken for dead and been buried alive. I would wake up from these utterly realistic dreams in my own bed. In the silence of the night with my heart pounding, covered with sweat, and unable to breathe for terror, I would still be convinced that I was enclosed in such a smothering blackness as I met on the Flint River, in a narrow coffin, locked down and closed tight without a speck of light or a single sound, far below the surface of the earth.

Considering these dreams and their connection with the dark, it is not surprising that sleep came hard to me. Still, it wasn't only dreams I feared at night. From somewhere I can no longer remember, perhaps from an overheard conversation between my parents, from something I read in a book, or from a snatch of news on the radio that sat in the living room by the door to the kitchen, I had conceived the idea that the world was full of men— "robbers" I called them to myself—waiting every night in the dark to scale the outsides of the apartment buildings of little girls, climb in their windows, and, while their parents slept in the next room, stab them dead.

An anonymous robber would want to do this, of course, because he so particularly hated girl children. I don't believe I ever wondered why a robber would hate small females of the species; I'm sorry to say that I think I took it for granted that we were naturally worthy of being hated. Instead, I tried to plan out how I might protect myself in the middle of the night against the inevitable invader. In addition to covering myself with stuffed animals, I decided that the best I could do was to make myself invisible. I would lie on my stomach as flat as I could, the covers pulled over me as smooth as I could make them, in hopes of persuading him that I wasn't there at all. That I wasn't there at all, or that I would be abandoned forever in a place no one would ever find me: this, I believe, was the root of my childhood fear of darkness.

I participated in a terrifying game of hide-and-seek when I was about ten or so, still living in New York with my father, mother, my little brother, Fred, and my brand-new baby brother, Wesley. There were several families of children living on top of each other in the garden apartments where we lived, almost all boys. Usually no matter what the weather, the whole lot of us were sent outdoors to play in the keyhole shaped opening around which the two-story red-brick apartments were arranged. One day, however, when it truly was too cold to be outside, Larry's mom, the most easy-going and indulgent of the mothers, had allowed the whole gang of boys and the three girls into Larry's apartment to amuse ourselves.

We began in Larry's and his little brother's bedroom. There, some of the flannel-shirted, sneakered boys sat on the brown rug next to the bunk beds and traded baseball cards. The girls in their play-dresses, *compared* trading cards (a gender difference enforced by parents and children alike). A few others, including me, read avidly through Larry's enormous, good-smelling piles of *Batman, Archie, Porky Pig, Superman,* and *Bugs Bunny* comic books. The rest of the boys, who didn't have baseball cards and who didn't like to read, lay on the floor picking at the rust-colored edges of the cowboy bedspread that hung in their faces and taunting each other.

When all of us were bored out of our minds at last, someone suggested an indoor game of hide-and-seek. This should not have been a very promising idea in a space as small as this tiny, regularly laid-out, absolutely unmysterious three-bedroom apartment. There were no hiding places except the obvious and few even of them. Still, the game promised us a chance to run in the house, a forbidden activity, to make noise, and to horse around and bang into one another before Larry's mother inevitably threw us out.

I liked the idea of playing hide-and-seek in the house, but I knew when we were outside I often was the one assigned the undesirable job of looking for the others who were hiding from me. Needless to say, I was greatly relieved to discover that this time, because it was his house, Larry was going to have to be "it." Larry went into the hall between two of the bedrooms, faced into the corner, closed his eyes, and covered his face by leaning his head against his arms; then he began to count to a hundred.

"One, two, three, four . . ."

Muffling giggles or poking one another irritably, most of the other children scattered quickly into the easy-to-find places, slithering under the bottom mattress of the bunkbed, jumping behind the shower curtain in the bathroom, crouching behind the couch, or lying down flat on a step in the stairwell.

"Thirty-one, thirty-two, thirty-three, thirty-four . . ."

I found myself paralyzed by fear. What if I couldn't find a place and I got caught unhidden, simply standing in the middle of the living room? The very idea of being shamed in this way would make my mind, always a bit slower than everyone else's, quit entirely.

By the time Larry had counted up to eighty-two everyone else had found a place to hide. I had to make myself move. From where I stood, I could see that there was room beside Kevin Oates behind the couch. As I jumped down next to him, he gave me a shove.

"You're breaking the rules," he hissed, outraged. "No sharing!"

I leaped back at once and wildly looked around the room. I could see a closed door! I had no idea where it went, but I opened it, rushed through it and pulled it closed behind me. I had shut myself in a closet. In the first moments, the relief of escape was overwhelming, but the relief was gone almost before it came. As I fell into the damp wool coats, the leggings, scarves, gloves, and mittens of Larry's alien household, I found myself swallowed up in the darkness of my dreams. I could still hear faint shouts and laughter on the other side of the door, yet I knew for a fact that I was already lost. The cramped closet in which I had shut myself had separated itself from the rest of the household and had already set out to travel into empty space, the worst nightmare of my imagination. If I couldn't leave immediately, I was lost.

I had to save myself. My feet entangled in the cast-off rubber boots and children's shoes that littered the floor beneath me, I managed to turn around to face the front of the closet. Gasping for air, I slapped my hands against the hollow wooden door and fumbled for the smooth brass handle with the locking button in the middle. I found the knob at last, turned it and flung myself into the light, panting with relief as the gang of boys ran up to me.

"You gave yourself away," they cried, jumping around me, leering with excitement. "Ha, ha, ha! We know where you were!" Hardly caring that I had so spectacularly lost the game, I looked with wonder past them at the bright, human room filled with couches and chairs, lamps and tables into which I had stepped. I wasn't gone forever after all; I still belonged to the world. My lungs filled up with air and my eyes with light. I was out of the closet. For now, I had escaped the darkness.

Two years later I remember being enclosed in darkness, swallowed up by its suffocating thickness with no hope this time of being saved, for it was an adult darkness springing from a grown-up knowledge, and I was still a child.

It was the darkness of grief, and I entered it my first night on my grandmother's farm in Kentucky immediately after the official end of my parents' marriage. Their divorce had been finalized the morning before at the courthouse in Jacksonville, Florida, following a very long train trip from Delaware. Having driven from Kentucky for the purpose, Aunt Kas and Uncle A.D. arrived in Florida shortly afterward to pick up a traumatized woman, two traumatized children, and a baby and take them "back home," as Mama said, to her own mother and father in Union County.

The divorce was not a surprise; at least it shouldn't have been. For the two preceding months I had stood around helplessly shifting from one foot to another while our house in Delaware was dismantled before my eyes. I watched in disbelief as dishes were packed, toys thrown away, mirrors taken from the walls to prepare for the movers. I had heard my mother cry. I had seen her put her head on my father's shoulder and sob as he held her. I had watched her purse up her mouth and refuse to answer my forbidden question, "Why, Mama, why?"

Even so, I had never truly believed that we could go so far, that my father would move to another house I hadn't even seen. As imaginative as I was, I wasn't able to imagine what it would actually feel like definitively to be without my father until bedtime that first night on the farm.

My father, my dear father! How hard it had been to be his child throughout my childhood! He was an extraordinary man who filled up a room with his presence. He was always the center of attention, even in the family. He was intellectually brilliant, vibrating with exuberant, cheerful energy, a cover-to-cover reader of the *New York Times,* a passionate lover of race cars and racing, Manhattan-cynical about almost everything and everybody, a despiser of the female, though amazingly good-looking and mesmerizingly charming to women, especially to the small one who happened to be his daughter. In our household, there was an absolute class system. He, the man, made up the ruling class; my mother and we children, the ruled. Though I nearly always resented it, the division made sense to me. Everything in the air spoke to me of the power of men, the weakness of women, but even apart from the general order of the universe, there was that specific to our family: it was my father's existence that gave the rest of us being, for he was the sun who shone within our walls, the star without whose presence there could be no life at all.

Apart from my father's charismatic glory, he was an old-fashioned man who had learned his child-rearing theories from his German mother and his even more German grandfather. He loved his children; there is no doubt about that, but he didn't really believe that children should be limited in their abilities in the way every one of them is. He expected in all things both adult perfection from us and unquestioning, never-talking-back, no-whining obedience. I not only feared his punishments, I was terrified of displeasing him and losing his love, and my fear coupled with my inability to please filled me alternately with hopelessness and fierce anger. Still, I loved him as passionately and as absolutely as I raged against him. He was unfair, but I had always thought he was the most wonderful human being who had ever lived, certainly the only one whose opinion of me mattered.

It was only that first night in Kentucky when I began to undress for bed in my grandmother's big, cold back room that I began to understand that the sun had permanently set, that my father really and truly had gone away forever. My father did not want any of us anymore; he would not have us. What had happened? I was eleven years old. The only sense I could make of it was this: he had gone at last because he was finally fed up with the dark planet who was his daughter.

I couldn't think how I was going to be able to live, with him moved back to New York and what was left of me there in Kentucky, thousands of miles away. I tried to will myself back into some kind of life among the living as I climbed up from the dark braided rug my grandmother and great-aunts had made, and into my side of the high wooden bed under the back window that faced out across the fields toward the distant Dyer Hills.

I burrowed down between the soft old sheets as I pulled up the thick layer of quilts that had been made for that very bed by my grandmother and my great-grandmother. One of those quilts was of silk, constructed from discarded men's ties laid out in a circle; another from large squares of brown, dark blue, and maroon wool salvaged from worn-out dresses and suits. They were the ugliest things I'd ever seen, and I hated both of them so much my stomach hurt. They were the work of women, the color, the texture, and the weight of what my father had rejected.

That night, as I waited in despair for my mother to tuck me in, I listened to her soft, anxious sounds as she put my brothers to bed next door in the little rickety room that had been the cold room in olden days when the back bedroom had been the kitchen. Once I heard my older brother cry out for my father; after that my mama's voice hushing him and petting him.

At last, exhausted, she came and absently kissed me goodnight as I clung to her neck. Then she straightened her back and went out, and I was truly alone. The dim overhead light was out and the doors shut. The air of the room still smelled faintly of the gas heater that had been turned off with the lights. I buried my head into the good soft pillows my grandmother had made from the down she had plucked from her own squealing geese, and tried to sleep.

I couldn't do it. Panicky, I lay there in the dark for hours, my stomach hurting and my body sore as I thought about my father and the fact that I would not see him again for a whole year. I already missed him so much I could hardly stand it. I turned it around and around to try to wear the edges of this sharp fact smooth, to make sense of it, to make it all right, but I could not. I was not quite twelve years old, and I was in darkness darker than what I would ever experience more than forty years later on the Flint River. A year from now was so long that I couldn't believe that it would actually ever come, and anyway, what would happen when it did? My father would still not want me.

A long time after that, my mother came back into what from now on would be our shared room. She did not turn on the light. I heard her undressing, laying her clothes on my grandmother's old rocking chair as she took off her wilted garments, one by one. There was a rustling as she dropped her nightgown over her head, then she climbed into the big bed beside me. Soon I could feel her trying to make herself a nest in which to get comfortable. I offered her no sympathy; she was a woman, along with me, a female and a child, a member of the failed underclass. Though I blamed myself, that night I blamed her, too. With a hard heart, I held myself still, pretending to be asleep. There was nothing I wanted to say to her, nothing she could offer me that mattered. Mother fell asleep quickly, though all through the rest of that dark night and through many nights to come I heard her moaning and whimpering as she slept beside me.

Whether I myself ever went to sleep after my mother came to bed I couldn't say. Perhaps I dozed a little; I have no memory of it if I did. What I remember most from the rest of those long, thick hours are the darkness and its silence. I had only lived in cities, first in New York and then in Wilmington, Delaware. Cities are hardly ever really dark and never completely quiet, even in the dead of night. Human light from gas stations and streetlights, from passing cars and faraway trucks puts a glow into the sky, and that glow faintly seeps in around the edges of window shades and watches over you.

As for the noises, in a city if you lie there long at night, alone and unable to sleep, you can almost always pick out the soothing sounds of traffic, the soft whoosh of the tires of a car on distant asphalt, as well as more domestic sounds—the banging of a garbage truck, someone calling to a dog or yelling at his wife or slamming a door down the block—to let you know that the world is still inhabited, that you, all alone in your bed, are not the last one alive on earth.

Night on the farm was mitigated by none of these comforts in those days before the advent of arc lights, when farmers and their families rose early and nobody drove their battered pickup trucks much after eight or nine o'clock in the evening. Besides the stars and a sometimes sickly, sometimes relentless moon, there were no shifting lights, no muffled glow, nothing human to brighten a room. Except for wind, rustling trees, and the occasional sound of an animal outside thrashing in the winter grass or grunting in its sleep, there was no noise at all.

I am not truly sure that that first night away from my father was the longest of my life since there were so many long ones that year and in the years to come. There were a lot of them around the time of my own divorce when I wondered whether I would be able to support my children. There were even more, the next year when I moved with them to Atlanta, more still years later as I lay in a cold sweat in the dark, worrying about what would happen to my adolescent daughter.

Though by then the quality of my darkness had utterly changed, I am very sure that two of my longest nights occurred six months before I turned fifty. They were the grief-filled nights immediately following my beloved father's death—my father to whom I had been able to return after so many years of estrangement, my father who had loved me with a loyal, innocent love in his last years of illness, my father who wanted me and was proud of me and had become my friend. Whatever the dread quality of the alien darkness and creeping silence of my childhood suffering, those later two nights were very nearly endless. That, however, is another story.

Back in my grandmother's bed that first night in Kentucky without my father, the earliest hint that the physical darkness that had swallowed me would cease came long before the dawn. It was not the familiar human noise of milk trucks and newspaper boys delivering papers; it was the alien sound of mourning doves singing their songs of grief as they perched on a branch of the bare tree outside our window. It was the worst sound on earth. "Oooo, ooo, oo, oooooo" I heard one sing. Its voice trailed away in despair, and another one answered it, "Oooo, oo, oo, oooo."

Throughout the night I had not cried once; now I turned over on my skinny stomach, wrapped my arms around my grandmother's pillows, pressed my face into their soft depths, and soaked them through with tears. I shook and gulped, sniffling and coughing. I tried to be quiet, as I attempted to hold my body still so that I would not wake my sleeping mother, who moaned and sighed beside me.

In the darkness the doves mourned and I cried, mourning with them. I mourned for my father; for my friend Susan Cagle, who moved away when I was nine, for other children I knew who didn't like me; for my step-grandmother, who disapproved of every breath I took; for my inability to learn in school; for my failures at home; for my mother's fear, grief, and distraction; for my inability to be like other children; for my own questions and doubts, pain, and anger, none of which I could find a way to express.

I mourned the loss of safety, of accustomed food, of the sight of skyscrapers on the way to my grandfather's apartment in Manhattan, of my familiar places, of any place where I would ever again belong.

I mourned the inevitable death of my mother (which I knew very well no well-meaning adult could promise me would not take place until I was an old woman), the death of my father, who was already gone anyway. I mourned the distant old man's death of my little brother Fred, whom I remembered with anguish eating an ice-cream cone, his cheeks and mouth covered in melted chocolate as he earnestly and unsuccessfully tried to learn to lick. I mourned my own death, too, my burial in the blind, cold ground I dreamed of, and my being forgotten, like every other human being who had ever lived and was now gone without a trace. In that early morning to the sound of doves I kept on crying and crying until I think there were enough tears to rust out my grandmother's ancient bathtub in the room next door.

Still, I could not stop crying, for soon my tears were no longer for myself and those I loved. They were for the suffering of all human beings who hurt, for the pain of little dying children going all alone into black emptiness, for fathers sent away from home to be killed in war, for wives cast off by husbands like dirty laundry. I cried for suicides like the mother down our block in New York who hanged herself from a chandelier, and the children of suicides, like her little boy who found her hanging. I cried for orphans, for unwanted children, for doddering old people, for those who were driven by fear or sorrow, who were cold and had nothing to eat.

I sobbed and whimpered for the victims of deliberately inflicted pain which I could not understand, for boys and girls bullied by other boys and girls, for Jews taken out of their homes and tortured—actually tortured!—and killed in the concentration camps about which I only heard adults speak in whispers, for Japanese children who did not look like me but who died from an atomic bomb dropped by my own country, and especially for the bewildered, mocked, and sneered-at men, women, and children who were called cruel, despising names—wops, broads, niggers, four-eyes, fatso, spicks, yankees, and worse—by others whose hatred was terrifying partly because I couldn't understand the reason for it and partly because I didn't know what anybody—including myself—could do to escape from it.

And then I grieved over all the rest of what I thought I knew as life: the deaths of helpless animals with which I identified far more than with any human beings, for dogs hit by cars, for cats torn to shreds by dogs, for birds swallowed down by cats. I grieved for pigs led to slaughter, for fish belly-up in an aquarium, for a fox shot by my uncles the previous summer, for ants stepped on by careless feet. I grieved for the last dinosaur before they all became extinct. I grieved for leaves falling from the trees, for stones kicked aside on a path, for the electric lightbulb turned off at the wall, for water running down the drain, even for the ground itself, cracked open by an earthquake, stamped on by careless feet, plowed and paved, stripped and plundered.

In the darkness of that morning as I lay in bed grieving for my father, I mourned creation itself, the shape of reality, the very fact of life for animate and inanimate things, the mortality of every single being that died, fell apart, rotted, wore down, came to an end. Nothing was left out of my mourning. In the whole world there was nothing left for celebrating, no goodness or happiness I could even imagine that could make up for such loss and pain.

And God? Where was God in all this misery? That early morning in my grandmother's bed, I don't think it occurred to me to wonder. Certainly, I wouldn't have thought God was grieving with me. I had heard enough times in Sunday school over the years that "death came through Adam," and "the wages of sin is death"; I suppose if I'd been forced to wonder by a grown-up's unlikely question, I would have said that God was probably sitting back watching all this suffering and death and saying, "I warned you that if you sinned, you would die. This is what you asked for, so I gave it to you."

Then, again, having no other way to conceive of God except as "heavenly Father," and therefore like my human father only bigger, I might have said that just as my own father got fed up with me and left, our heavenly Father, who was in every way perfect and attractive, also got fed up and left. Why, after all, should he want to be bothered with anyone or anything so small, insignificant, imperfect, and boring as we, the human and nonhuman components of his creation?

Human beings suffered, grieved, and died alone, and that was all there was to it. This is what it meant to be human; I'd worked it out myself, and since I had been the smallest child I had been crushed by the weight of it. The fact is, I really didn't much wonder why things were the way they were; few of the things adults did or thought ever made sense to me or seemed fair, and God, of course, was the biggest adult of all. Whatever the reason was for the suffering I could see, I was smart enough to know that, whatever the unlikely promises of heaven, there was nothing on this earth that could be done about any of it.

No, I'll have to say, I never really wondered why things were as they were. For years, my questions were altogether different. They were these: why didn't anybody else, adult or child, seem to see the reality and pervasiveness of death that I could not avoid seeing? And, why, whenever I tried to talk about what I saw, were the grown-ups as well as the children so alarmed? What was it in my words that made them angry? Why did they shut me up as though I had said or done something obscene?

It was dark that night on the Flint River. My childhood darkness was much darker, an altogether different kind of darkness.

I remembered it all that long wet night more than forty years later as I clumped and stumbled along behind my friend, expecting to die, preparing to die in that dark so deep that I couldn't see my hand before my face. I wondered and I kept on wondering: when my child's heart had been cracking in two with the loneliness and terror of what I knew, why had I been sent into the wilderness alone?

Mercifully, Pam at last interrupted my brooding by speaking to me.

"Time for a break," she called out cheerfully. Still holding the back of her coat, I could feel her fumbling around with her paddle to find a log the three of us could sit on while we shared our last swallows of water.

Still under the influence of those ancient memories, I plopped down on the log beside her without answering. She knew immediately that something was wrong. "Are you okay, Bobbie?" she asked. She put the plastic jug in my hands and an arm around my shoulders.

Gently, her question brought me to where I actually was. I could still hear gunshots. I was exhausted, sore from head to foot, the things that had come back to me from my childhood had left me bruised, and my eyes so hurt from straining through the darkness that they throbbed, and I continued to believe I, at least, would soon die, but I was not alone. When I listened, I could hear the soft human sound of the "whoosh, whoosh" of tires on a road somewhere; Jeff was silent, but he was there; Pam, my friend, was beside me, and there was God, filling the darkness with God's immediate, intimate presence.

Was I all right? So what if I expected I would die? In gratitude so profound it hurt my chest, the memory of the gifts of my life gathered themselves up from my childhood tears and fell like rain into a deep well of joy.

I drank my share of the water gratefully, passed on the bottle to Jeff, and folded my hands together to stretch my fingers, which had grown cramped around the handle of my wooden paddle.

"I'm fine, Pammy," I answered with surprise. "I'm just fine."

Star

As we sat there on our log, Pam, Jeff and I, absorbing our meager mouthfuls of water, we began to feel the chill seeping slowly into the backs of our legs. For a while we were silent as we listened to the fading but comforting sounds of traffic on a far-off road and the sporadic gunshots of drunken hunters. The close-up noises, too, rose up invisibly from the wet woods like a mist from the ground, the drip, drip of water on a rock, the creaking and thrashing in soggy leaves of a larger animal rooting in the ground behind us, the squeaking and sighing of many unidentified small ones hunted by night-seeing owls and coyotes.

We could see nothing, yet the longer we sat there the more we heard. Indeed, there was too much to hear, too little to see in that utter darkness. It was disorienting, to say the least—an odd experience of sensory overload laid on top of sensory deprivation.

"I wonder what time it is?" Pam broke our human silence at last.

I coughed a little as I cleared my dry throat. "I don't

know," I answered. "I keep holding my watch up to my face, but it never does any good. I can't even see my hand, much less the time. It certainly feels odd after all these hours not being able to tell if it is closer to nine o'clock or to midnight."

Jeff, who was nursing his knee and had hardly moved since we sat down, unexpectedly spoke up. "It's about nine," he said. "I'm sure it's not later than that."

Was he telling us not to whine, things weren't as bad as we were making them out to be? Or did he really think it wasn't late? Neither of us asked him, and Jeff lapsed back into silence.

Now I could hear Pam patting restlessly at her pockets. I knew what she was looking for. She was aware there was nothing left to eat. Nevertheless, my friend loves camping gadgets; even in town she generally has two or three tucked away somewhere on her person.

"Pam, you've been through your pockets a thousand times"; I was not too tired to tease her. "What do you expect to find in there?"

Pam surprised me by giving a deep sigh. For the first time I could see that she was worried about how we would get out.

"I wish I had my little flashlight," she answered. "Then we could read the compass I have around my neck."

"But Pam," I responded, in a sudden brief panic. "I thought you could see the animal trails along the edge of the river. Why do we need the compass?" I could not help recalling the way we had come thus far, the brooks we had forded which had seemed to be flowing into the main channel of the river. The Flint was extremely dried up and some of the streams had been quite far across. I had worried all along that we had somehow taken a wrong turn and were now following one of those streams instead. Now I understood that Pam might have been thinking this, too.

Before I could ask her what was on her mind, however, she gave a cry of excitement.

"Look what I found!" she said.

I couldn't see what it was she had dug out of some otherwise unmined pocket, of course, but I heard it soon enough. It was the shiny silver police whistle that all the women at our university had been issued a few years ago when there was an attempted rape on campus. The idea was that, if we believed we were in some kind of danger, we were to blow the whistle to summon help as well as to frighten away our attackers. It was so loud that it was obvious why it was illegal to blow it in town without good reason.

Pam took a deep breath. "I always wanted to do this," she said. "Tweeeee, tweeee, tweee." Pam blew until my eyes watered and my ears hurt.

I didn't want to dim her exuberance, but I couldn't stand much more of it. "Pam, stop," I shouted when I could take it no longer. "Nobody can hear us out here; you're just wasting good breath."

She blew a few more blasts as I clamped my hands over my ears to dull the noise, which was amazingly high as well as being simultaneously piercing and meaty.

She stopped for a moment and panted. "Got to blow it till somebody comes," she said.

"Pam," I answered, reasonably, "nobody can hear your

whistle, but even if they could, they'd never be able to get to us to get us out of this jungle. How would they see to find us?"

"They can send a helicopter!" she replied. She blew again a time or two, then I heard her zipping her pants pocket (or whichever pocket it was) and the whistle was gone.

I didn't say anything more, but after a moment she sighed again and slapped the top of her legs. "Well," she said, "we'd better get walking if we're going to get Jeff out of here before his knee freezes up."

Soon, we were on our feet once more, Pam in front and Jeff in back, feeling our way slowly through the invisible tangled underbrush with the blades of our paddles. The withered vines sucking at my legs like the tentacles of some amphibious, skinny-legged monster, I crept along inch by inch. The rest had done me good; I was tired, but not as much as I would have expected. My body hurt—legs, hands, feet, shoulders and chest—but the pain was not unbearable. It was a good time, indeed, the first time on the trip I had really been able to mull over the life I had had as well as to consider the people with whom I had shared it who were dear to me, most especially my mother and father, my children, and above all, Richard, my husband and companion.

As for my parents, my father was dead. On my side, it had been a painful relationship. From my childhood until well into my forties he was the person in my life who had stood closest to the center of my imagination at the same time I had been convinced that I meant nothing to him. Now I let myself be flooded with the gratitude which was already always present in me for the gifts of the healing of our relationship and our friendship in his last years.

I thought of my mother, too, with love and gratitude, remembering the hard years of my raising when she so struggled both to support my brothers and me and to instill in us a desire to "make something" of ourselves. When I was a young woman it had been painful to disappoint her with my terrible housekeeping and my other social failures, but how much she had wanted for me, and how much she had loved and given and supported me in return! Now, my mother was elderly but she was also strong. My death would be a terrible thing for her; still, surrounded by my brothers and their families as well as by my own children, she would not be alone.

Then, there were my children. Anna Grace and Benjamin were both grown, and this, too, filled me with gratitude. For years I had suffered the terror of imagining that something like this would happen to me before they left home. They had suffered through the end of my first marriage with all its miseries and disruptions as well as the hard years preceding it. If I were to die, I worried that they would lose not only me, but Richard, who loved them as his own but had never been able to adopt them legally. Though a person never stops needing her or his mother—how could I have managed even over the past few years without my own mother?—it was an enormous relief that they had got out of childhood to adulthood without these losses.

After that came the thought of Richard, and here, for the first time, I felt a pang so sharp it was like a pain in my side. For a moment I could hardly breathe. My husband would not be sitting quietly, calmly contemplating and evaluating our past marriage or his future suffering. He, of all these people I loved, was the only one who knew I was in danger as well as something of the nature of that danger. Whatever he was feeling—fear and anguish, alternating restless anxiety and helplessness, hope and grief—for him during this long night alone there would be no compensation in the thought of work completed or love lived out, no ease, no consolation for my imagined death either in the memory or the knowledge of the happiness of our life together. For him, as for me, there was so much to remember known only to ourselves, shared kindness and passion, beauty and sorrow, and underlying everything else, pure, unalloyed joy. Oh Richard! In that moment his beautiful face with its green eyes and gentle mouth gleamed in the darkness before me, and there was nothing I could do but to close my eyes to it.

Deliberately, I turned my mind away from my husband. I began instead to consider the work I had done in my life, and it was a relief to contemplate.

Not that my past had been crowned by successes: with an emotional effort I might otherwise not have been willing to make, I thought of the sad and angry years of my adolescence when I had not been able to imagine how I as a woman could live a life in which I could thrive. I considered my much longer years of college, graduate school, and young womanhood while I was married, during which I aimed desperately at a life of teaching and writing that the world of which I was a part told me I had no right to attain.

I remembered how I had tried to give over my life at eighteen, convinced as I was that, in spite of my husband's mistrust and even dislike of me, I might as well marry and get it over with. I thought of the ways I had withered up under the continual, unanswerable anger of this same husband because of what he considered to be my failures as a wife and later, as a mother.

I remembered my childhood and adult depression that had kept me quiet, though hardly docile, through all the long period in which everything I could not help being was in conflict with everything that was being asked of me. It was a depression that choked me and battered me into alternating periods of quiet and desperate, shaming speaking from the time before I was in kindergarten until one Easter weekend when I was forty-eight years old. This was when I came to understand in my prayer all the complex parts of my depression. "The joy of the resurrection renews the whole world": there, on Good Friday, by some miracle of grace God's mercy drenched my soul with rain, so that I could answer it and grow up through it like fresh wheat. So was I healed of it.

Most of all, I remembered my attempts to learn to speak, though not the kinds of words and sentences we learn as children that are more designed to distract, conceal, and mislead than to speak the truth, which is beautiful and good simply by virtue of being true. I recalled the child I was, trying to talk about the obscene, hidden things of life. There were the things of darkness—my knowledge of the inevitability of death for every living being; the probability of "them" dropping the atomic bomb on "us"; my fears and ongoing depression, which I didn't understand; later, my parents' divorce, the meaninglessness of human life as I saw it then, and the meanness and malice that seemed to govern so much of the time spent with my peers; the mysterious, often troubling relationship between my aunt who was my father's sister and my father, as well as between my father's mother and my mother; and on top of everything else, why so much was forbidden to women and why I, as a female child, had to obey my elders without talking back, respecting them, accepting their punishments, and taking their criticisms to heart, no matter what they happened to be.

There, stumbling along behind Pam on the slippery bank of the Flint River, I remembered, too, trying unsuccessfully to find a way to speak of what I loved or yearned for without angering, boring, or embarrassing the grown-ups around me. I longed to describe the beauty of light shining through the delicate pale green leaves of early spring; the gleam of soft black fur on the stomach of the cat I imagined would be my very own; the shape of the melodies of flute and oboe in *Peter and the Wolf*; the ineluctable, utterly satisfying soul-and-body combination of rhythm, sound, and visual images; the comfort and surprise in certain poetry.

It seems to me now, as it seemed to me then, that the very sound of my voice oddly angered most of the people with whom I shared my life—first my parents and teachers and then my classmates. Later, it was my first husband whom I offended in this way. To him, my voice was so ugly, embarrassing, and destructive that if anyone should pay attention to it, he believed it would undermine the very social order.

"Did you know you make a fool of yourself every time you open your mouth to talk about something that isn't the early church?" he told me once in a kindly voice. I had said something theologically stupid at a party we had both attended; he hoped that his warning would prevent future social discomfort. Self-consciously, for years afterward, at parties, conferences, and faculty meetings I remembered what he told me and I kept a watch over my mouth.

Slowly, systematically, and sadly, then, I learned to mute my voice until I became able to speak only of the things that mattered to me in my head, and even then I could only half believe that the things I spoke about to myself were not crazy.

Yet it was an ability to meet reality with words that I craved as a child and as a young adult—precise words, delicate, hinting phrases made of words, solid metal sentences of words, rhythmic paragraphs of words, words so beautiful that when I wrote them on a page or spoke them, they would find the very place where light and sound become indistinguishable from each other. What I wanted was to let the reality I saw, felt, and tasted come up from my body and through my lips in the form of words—spoken words; real, absolutely fearless words; words of substance and strength. I wanted words that would draw me into being with them and connect me to all that was—earth, light, water, love, other people. In short, I craved words; I craved God who is, indeed, the Word.

In the beginning was the Word, and the Word was with God, and the Word was God. [The Word] was in the beginning with God. All things came into being through [the Word], and without [the Word] not one thing came into being. What has come into being in [the Word] was life, and the life was the light of all people. The light shines in the darkness, and the darkness did not overcome it. (John 1:1-5)

I am not sure when it was that I first fully understood that I myself as a woman and as a human being am an expression of the Word who is God. It should have been possible to have learned it in Sunday school if my city Sunday school back then in the fifties hadn't been so determinedly rationalist. Don't get me wrong, however; after Pond Fork Baptist Church's hellfire-and-damnation summer revivals, I liked our church just fine. We didn't talk theology in the Methodist Church in those days beyond the things that distinguished us from the Presbyterians (they believed in "predestination" over against "free will"), the Baptists (they believed in the inerrancy of scripture and "once saved, always saved" rather than in "backsliding and repentance"), and from the utterly godless, idol-worshiping, pope-rather-than-conscience-obeying, you-can-do-anything-you-want-if-you-just-confess-it-to-a-priest-later Roman Catholics (they believed in "works righteousness" as opposed to our saving belief in "justification by faith").

I know that from a young age I had a very strong sense of the relationship between the transitory beauty of real individual lives, including my own, and the firm, eternal reality of what I would later learn from the early church to call God the Word which lay under, gave shape to, and supported not only those lives but everything which is.

> Under the transparent water color
>> which is me,
> I see in part the penciled black line
>> of eternity.
> The ever guide—the design of the complexity,
>> The circular unwashable infinity.

When I ponder this poem I so clearly remember writing from my gut when I was seventeen, I still wonder where this knowledge of the Word came from.

I remember with astonishment something that took place the next winter when I was eighteen after I was married and living in corrugated-iron graduate student barracks apartments (my husband was a graduate student in chemistry at Iowa State University, and so I had transferred there for my second year in college). I was walking home alone from some event or other that had taken place on campus. It was deep night, and it was a long way. New snow lay on the ground so thick that it threatened and sucked at my freezing toes in their skimpy boots. In my thin black and white coat left over from high school in a warmer clime, I felt like a bewildered child, shivering and blowing out my breath into my gloved hands as I stamped along on the unshoveled sidewalk, pretending that the steam I made was real steam which could warm me.

About a half mile from home, walking past the great, silent barns of the agricultural college, I looked up and saw the stars, and immediately I was carried out of my late childhood miseries into another place of wonder and power. The stars were stars as I had never seen them before. In that clear dark night, they were alive with a nonhuman presence. They shone equally in that deepest blue sky on the white snow and the black trees, and they shone with such light, with such a passionate intensity that they seemed to hum and vibrate at the very place where light becomes indistinguishable from music.

The cold and my inadequate winter clothes completely forgotten, I stopped and stood still under those stars, my face to the sky, listening and wondering with my whole being as I tried to absorb the sounds that so thoroughly coincided with this heavenly light. Then, suddenly, I moved from the place of what I saw and heard to a place right through it: I sensed, seeing and feeling in my mind, my fingers, and my bones the strong and delicate lines of energy connecting the stars with each other and with our world, the construction and the movement of atoms within molecules, the patterns of the hibernation of animals, the austere and shining life of numbers within their formulas. In short, the skinny, freezing, demoralized girl I was, standing there on the middle of that frozen path, jaw dropped, was given a glimpse of the structures of all things, all things which are good and beautiful because they are an expression of God.

Reflecting on it later, did I know in that moment that I had seen for myself the spoken word of the yet for me unspoken Word of God, God who creates all things, orders all things, heals all things that are broken, and resurrects all things? Somehow, though I would never have thought to connect it with what I heard about in church, I believe I did.

If I didn't know it then, three years later in seminary I recognized with astonishment what I had known as a child and what I had seen in that winter sky in Iowa in the writers of the early church I now teach, writers like Justin Martyr, Irenaeus, and Origen, all of whom spoke of the God we are able to know and experience in the human and the nonhuman natural world about us, the God who is revealed in all things, the God in whose image our very minds are made, as God the Word. It was this Word, they believed, who was incarnate in Jesus Christ, the Word made flesh about whom I was already certain the opening verses of John were speaking! I was not alone.

The one of whom they spoke and the one I knew already in my own deepest experience were one and the same: God the Word, spoken out of the silence; God the Word, whose silent image, whose image darkened by silence I was!

I enjoyed my graduate work at Oxford, although none of it was easy. Languages come hard for me, yet for my first degree I studied not theology (how could I trust its God?) but ancient Semitic languages, Hebrew, Syriac, and Aramaic. Though they were not my words, I loved the alien, ancient texts. At the same time, what I had begun to learn in seminary about the Word who gave meaning and substance to all words began to fade from my mind. Tutorials those first few years were difficult beyond belief as I sat with my tutor in that great place of centuries of learning, in a closed room discussing my weekly translations and essays. I was so overcome by shame at the very sound of my own voice that it drove every thought from my brain and made me quiver with fear.

Yet, I delighted in my years there. The golden stone of Oxford, the brilliant secret gardens of its colleges, the red cows in Christ Church Meadow, the swarms of men on bicycles from the Morris Works, the Cherwell River slipping underneath the willows in University Parks, an old-fashioned friend whose father had been killed in World War II and so was raised by his grandfather who was a veteran of World War I, a pickled human heart collected in Cornwall this century and preserved in the Pitt-Rivers Museum, the choir boys singing like a memory of angels from the top of Magdalen College tower in the sweet dawn of May Morning, the rustling summer trees of St. Giles, the soft and searing spires and towers of the ancient buildings that lined the curving High Street, the tomb of St. Frideswide, the pure blue of sky, the depth of ancient shadows—on certain days I felt myself to be so flooded with this pulsing, pushing, painful beauty that I choked and spluttered in it, gasping and swallowing it down like a drowning woman saving herself by drinking.

There was little comfort in my third year in Oxford as I looked for a dissertation topic. Classes and tutorials were over as well as exams. Cast up out of the light and roads and company of all that beauty, for months I sat stunned and mute in the dingy oriental reading room of the New

Bodleian Library, poring over what I could now see were the ugly, pompous, and judgmental ancient Christian texts to which I had consigned five years of my life by having chosen to do my research in Syriac patristics. Believe me, it was a bad season, a cold and rainy season in which I was all alone.

Then, one day in that dim, dirty-windowed place, the Word, who is ever merciful and loves humankind, brought me face-to-face once more, not with the terrifying, judging God I'd been taught about in my childhood, but with the Word, God's own self who slowly and secretly had continued to be shown to me from the time I was a little girl.

Shuffling during a dreary afternoon through the enormous piles of books on the desk before me, I picked up a late-nineteenth-century volume entitled *The Thirteen Ascetical Volumes of Philoxenus of Mabbug*. Languorously, I flipped open the red-leather-spined book to its thick middle, and there, from that page written for the instruction of sixth-century monks, the Word leaped out to me, like Christ leaping down to the prisoners in hell.

Monks should not pass judgment or otherwise criticize one another, said Philoxenus to me from that page. Rather, Christians should treat those around them with the gentle compassion of God. Be like God, Philoxenus said, God who longs for human thriving, who withholds judgment, who makes allowances, who—out of kindness—looks on those wordless with fear and says, "Do not be afraid to speak: be not afraid."

My ears were ringing and I could hardly catch my breath. In Philoxenus' text that rainy afternoon, I knew at once that I was listening to the beating heart of early monastic theology, and it was beating for me, not only to the forgotten music of the Word spoken by Irenaeus, Justin, and Origen when I had met them in seminary. It was the same rhythm to which the stars were vibrating in the night sky of Iowa so many years before. I calmed myself as best I could, and committed myself at once to write on Philoxenus' ascetic theology.

Unfortunately, I was not allowed to do it. Back in those days of miniskirts and the Beatles, bicycles, and dining halls to which women were not permitted, an ancient understanding of the Christian life was not regarded as a properly theological topic for scholarly research, and so I reluctantly committed myself instead to studying another topic in Philoxenus, the sixth-century Monophysite Christology for which he was better known. I am not blaming my teachers for what happened. If I could have answered those words of the Word, "be not afraid," and brought myself to fight for what I loved, they would have let me do what I wanted, but I could not speak. Words failed me.

And now my struggles really began. Though to produce a technical study of the Syrian branch of the Monophysites in the christological controversies of the early church felt well-nigh impossible to me, dispositionally speaking, I somehow knew that if I were to survive, I had no choice. Against myself, I threw myself wholeheartedly into a study of those texts.

Soon, I paid a heavy price for such wholeheartedness. I was a historian and not, I was convinced, a Christian, and yet hardly any time had passed before I discovered that for me to dive down without an oxygen tank into the depths of the fourth-, fifth-, and sixth-century writers on the nature and work of Jesus Christ was a frightening experience. Because I quickly came to care very deeply about what I discovered so far below the surface of those turbulent coral and snake-filled black waters, it was even more terrifying to try to write about what I found there.

It was almost three years, I remember, and many reams of paper later before I was able to type out a single paragraph I could use. My head was full of the intricate structures of classical Christology, aching to the bursting point with the powerful, secret words that described and controlled it. "Self-subsistent" and "non-self-subsistent hypostases," "physis," "natural union," "prosopon," "communicatio idiomatum," "schema," "ousia," "synapheia," "theoria"—I knew the precise meaning of each word in every writer, each word or phrase, Syriac, Greek, Latin or English, in its most technical sense as well as in its deepest sense at the level of faith. Still, it all existed in my head in a great shining ball of intertwined ideas and inarticulate feelings. I couldn't separate the strands in my brain to write it all down in any logical order, and, most painfully of all, to submit it to any other human eyes for judgment.

More than thirty years later, I don't recall whether there was a certain moment when I figured out well enough how to do the job actually to write my dissertation. What I do remember is sitting in my study at my typewriter, staring week after week as I got pregnant, gave birth, nursed a baby, then reared a small child, first at the texts on the desk beside me—texts I knew as well as the palms of my own hands—and then at the white sheet of paper curled up in the typewriter in front of me. After a long time, I would squeeze out a sentence or two, my heart pounding in terror, my stomach roiling. Then, unable to go on, I would read the words I had written, rip the page from the typewriter, ball it up in my hands and throw it into the pile of other balls just like it on the floor by the wastebasket.

I did finally get through my dissertation. I even published it with a good press. I had produced a scholarly piece of work, and I was proud of it. The Word was forgotten, my problems solved. I began at once to plan out my further scholarship. I completed an article on another set of ancient christological texts with which I had wrestled, and that was published, too. I sighed with relief. At least on paper I had broken through the terrors that had prevented my putting into words the things that mattered to me. If only it had been true!

I made a lot of changes in my life shortly after the publication of that article. I was divorced. I took a job several hundred miles away in a seminary where I was hired to teach, not Semitic languages, as I had been doing, but early Christian thought. A year later, I married Richard.

Among all these other changes I had made a decision: I needed to turn away from the technical, often abstract, and generally crotchety literature of the ancient christological controversies upon which I had been working the previous nine years to return to the ascetic, early monastic writings that had first drawn me into them in the dank oriental reading room of the Bodleian library while I was still a graduate student at Oxford.

Already, before I had moved south, I had expanded my interests beyond Philoxenus to begin not only to study but to live out of the words spoken by the great Abbas and Ammas of the fourth- through the sixth-century Egyptian Desert recorded in the *Sayings of the Fathers*. In various ways, as I had gone through the last years in the North, the words of these teachers had saved my life. They were not only telling me who God was as they insisted on the centrality of love in the Christian life, they were training me as a human being made in the image of God. They taught me feminism, encouraging me to be fearless, to take risks, as a woman as well as a scholar standing over against what was expected of me, which I never otherwise would have taken.

"Unless [a person] say in [her] heart 'in the world there is only myself and God,' [that person] will not find peace," said Abba Alonius to me as I had shaken with fear over my colleagues' supposed judgment on the new direction of my work. What else can you expect? Amma Syncletica said to me. "In the beginning there are a great many battles and a good deal of suffering for those who are advancing towards God and afterward, ineffable joy. It is like those who wish to light a fire; at first they are choked by the smoke and cry, and by this means obtain what they seek. . . . So we also must kindle the divine fire in ourselves through tears and hard work." If you expect to learn to speak, she went on, of course it will be hard and your eyes will water, but this will not be forever.

Both of them were right. Quickly, in the context of teaching at the seminary, I found myself forced to relate differently to these great teachers of the early church who had been and were still my most private companions. Now I had to go against my own calmly rationalistic seminary and Oxford training to seek ways to teach their texts that would allow them to speak to the students as they spoke to me.

If I were to share my understanding of the life-giving meaning of their words (as I would have to if I were to take my vocation as a teacher seriously, and if I were to be true to the Abbas and Ammas themselves), then I had to take the gag out of my own mouth and speak. Because the texts spoke of them, I had to learn to raise out loud in class the old topics that I still could hardly bring up publicly without fear, including the inevitability of death, the forces and emotions in each human psyche that keep us from loving, prayer, and the healing of our wounded psyches.

Bringing myself to speak the words in class, going against myself as well as my social and scholarly training, and enduring my own anxiety was hard and painful work. Mother Syncletica was right. There was, indeed, a lot of smoke and tears, and it took a long time, but I learned to do it.

When the time came, however, to begin writing books—putting on paper for other people's, other scholars' judgment—about what most mattered to me, it was something else. It took me five years to write the small book on early monastic spirituality in which I finally began not only to speak to others in print, but also to find a style of writing, a way of approaching the material that suited me, my imagined readers, and the ancient texts.

For a long time, as I had written my dissertation, I squeezed out each sentence in a torture of imagined judgment. Thinking of my modern teachers' and colleagues' disapproving faces, I suffered frequently from headaches, stomachaches, and backaches. I cried a lot and railed against my ancient teachers' insistence that I overcome my fears of saying what I saw, not by avoiding speaking but by doing it.

The fact was, however, the Abbas and Ammas were right. By the last chapter of that book, ideas occasionally came to me in words already shaping themselves into sentences; the writing was getting easier. For the second book, paragraphs sometimes rose up in my mouth to be written down. I suffered a setback with the book after that, in which I raised the old topics in ways overtly intimate to me, but the next, although it contained so much that was painful, was truly my words to the Word.

Words to the Word, my writing had become my prayer. "Teach your mouth to say that which you have in your heart," said Abba Poemen (Poemen 63). When I finished that particular book I was more than fifty years old. I believed I had learned to do it.

One day after all that, I made a surprising decision, at least it surprised me. It was time for me to begin an entirely different kind of book.

Have I said that I come from an amazing western Kentucky farm family on my mother's side? It is a tribe of powerful women, a matriarchy of which my grandmother Roberta, by virtue of being the oldest daughter of my great-grandmother Amma, used to be the head. My own mother, Mary, being the oldest daughter of my grandmother, inherited the position from her, and I, the least of all the generations of women, as my mother's oldest daughter, am set up, in a manner of speaking, to take over the position from her.

It was not a position I ever relished inheriting. For one thing, from the time we went to live on my grandparents' farm after my parents' divorce, I think I associated that whole side of my family with the loss of my father. Not being permitted to so much as hint at the divorce at a time when there was very little else on my mind, I was silenced among these female relatives of mine as I've rarely been before or after.

But this was not the whole of it. There were the strengths, virtues, and skills they embodied that I was meant to emulate: toughness; humor; hands and knees in the garden at dawn; willingness to work a sixteen-hour day seven days a week; an ability to cook anything without a recipe or, as far as I could see, without having been taught; loyalty to blood; refusal to speak about one's own negative feelings, especially depression; contempt of city softness; lack of squeamishness at the sight of blood, feathers, slime, or dirt; skills at sewing; and finally, "insensitivity" ("You're just too damn sensitive," my mother would tell me grimly when I would cry from being teased. I had made her break her own rule about swearing because I'd driven her to distraction).

All of these values, virtues, and even recipes, were conveyed to me against my will in stories of the lives and times of my mother's, grandmother's, and great-grand-mother's generations. As I cringed down, utterly empty of stories of my own, Mama, my aunts, and my great-aunts would tell them over and over again. Cooking their dinners, canning their beans, drinking iced tea in the gliders on their porches, cleaning their kitchens, they were never without tales.

As a child and even as a young adult, I felt battered by the words of those stories and the lives they shaped. If I could never live up to them, what did I care about the House on the Hill in which my mother and my grand-mother had been born, or how Great-great-aunt Lucy raised her sister's daughters, Mabel and Stella, to be her servants after their mother committed suicide? An awk-ward, lazy, and tongue-tied Yankee, I had none of the virtues of my aunts or my great-aunts, none of their skills or their hard-working dispositions. In terms of the fami-ly, I was a failure and I would always be a failure. How, knowing this, could I help hating those stories and those lives and feeling shamed by them?

Then, about the time the Abbas and Ammas began to give me words of my own to speak, these family tales became transformed for me. From the time I was a child, whatever else they had told me, they had always seemed to sit in judgment on me, on my failures, on my not belonging, and on the alien Yankee-ness of my blood. Now, all of a sudden I was able to hear them for what they were.

Certainly, they were not about me at all. Rather, they were stories of great beauty—intimate, funny, wonderful stories of the lives and ways of life of real women, children, and men long passed but to whom I was linked by blood. Human images of the Word, once these people had been strong, tough, skilled, and fierce, but by now nearly all of them were dead. Apart from the eternal memory of God, they existed only in the memories of those of us who still saw their faces or imagined them, and all were fragile, as delicate, heart-breaking, and beautiful as dry leaves in February.

It was clear to me now that both in my role as oldest daughter and as a lover of the Word, I was called to write their stories and preserve those memories in their beauty. Considering my relatives' reluctance to let knowledge of the unpleasant outside the bounds of family, I wasn't sure how I was going to be able to do it.

Astonishingly, my mother, my aunts, and my one remaining great-aunt were excited by the prospect. (Had anything I had done before seemed to my aunts to be worth doing? I had no memory of it.) In preparation for the writing, Mama endlessly called me from Louisville on the phone to tell me snips and pieces of her own memories; Great-aunt Blacky wrote down stories from her childhood; and, when I visited, Aunt Kas and Aunt Suzie told me more to fill out the already familiar stories, as well as to fill them in with the "grown-up" parts I'd never heard before. To think that one of my great-grandmother's sisters had an illegitimate baby she kept in the barn!

It was wonderful, even exhilarating. Nevertheless, soon, all of what they said to me was twisted round and round in a great ball with the yarns I remembered on my own, the things I had heard in childhood, what I had seen

114

for myself and felt, and most of all what I had worked out long ago about what was not allowed to be spoken or was only whispered.

When it came right down to it, except for bits and pieces here and there, I couldn't write it into a coherent whole. As I had not been able to do with my dissertation, I simply couldn't take the pieces apart and put them back together outside my mind. For four years I struggled to try to do it. I sat at the computer and tugged at the wisps of words and tail ends of sentences.

In the night I dreamed it. I dreamed of hair twisted into glossy buns, and the hems of sturdy dark dresses; I dreamed of plowed fields and sagging porches, of mockingbirds in cowslips and burning houses. In my dreams there were stories upon stories of shining words, and all of them true. In the daytime, I suffered from stomachaches, dry mouth, and fear. Once more, my words had failed me. After all this time, I was back in the dark where I was almost thirty years before, and the dark did not go away.

Then it was Christmas morning of my fifty-third year. There would be company for dinner—the children and some old family friends. Our household woke up early to the smell of the tree. Excited by the prospect of the day in front of us, Richard got up to make my coffee and read the paper before we got to the presents. Knowing I would be busy from the moment my feet touched the floor, I decided I had better have my prayers in bed.

A few minutes later Richard brought in the coffee and set it on the table beside me. I sat up, had three or four good swallows of it, and adjusted myself under the warm comforters against a pile of pillows. Then I closed my eyes and slowly drew in a deep Christmas breath.

I was not in the place I expected to be. Letting out the breath I had just drawn in, I found myself standing all alone inside a moist and pitch black tunnel that I could feel stretched out a long way before me and behind me.

As I stood there wondering where I was, suddenly the beam of a powerful light shone against the wall of the tunnel in front of me. Then, three things happened all at once. First, I knew where I was: I had become a giant esophagus, and I was standing inside it. Second, looking at its walls with recognition, I heard these words, "the light of Christ." Third, in that light of Christ I was able to understand something of what had been going on within me ever since childhood that I had never seen before.

I had, indeed, received everything that came to me as a giant hungry esophagus from childhood on. Rather than speaking of it, everything that happened to me, every experience I had, each book I read, all I saw, felt, smelled, touched, thought about, heard, and even tasted, I had shoveled or sucked up into myself, interpreting it, greedily swallowing it down, and absorbing the words of it into my body to hoard to myself and keep it safe from outside hands. I thought I couldn't tolerate the judgments on me if I spoke—yes, but there was more to it than that. The words I couldn't speak or write were the words I didn't want to give away.

This was a horrifying insight. As a child, there had been a reason for my hoarding: what I valued was devalued, and I was afraid. As a young adult woman I had had to continue my hoarding. The last thirty years of my life, however, had been spent trying to learn to speak out the words I had continued to swallow. No wonder writing was such a physical and emotional effort! The Abbas and Ammas speak of the need to go against yourself in order to grow in love; in order to write, to connect myself with God and the other people in my world, I had been going against myself in ways I had hardly fathomed.

"The Light of Christ!" On that Christmas morning it shone into my dark and ugly places with the focused intensity of a laser. That day what it meant for me that God should come among us, full of light and truth, was this: I would have to stand in that terrible, cleansing light. Was the revelation of the Word of God not only the disclosing of God's presence in creation, in the laws of nature, in the process of our own minds, but also the revelation to ourselves of everything in us that stands between us and the image of the Word we are created to be, of everything we must renounce and bring to God in order to be healed? For me, Christmas morning, it was.

I got up shortly from my prayer and, in spite of my better judgment considering all I had to do the rest of the day, sat down at my computer. The stories I had longed to write began to flow from me first in words, then in sentences and paragraphs.

All human life is a miracle, at the same time all nature is exactly what it is. "The Word became flesh and dwelt among us."[1] In Jesus Christ, "God became what we are in order that we become what God is," Athanasius said in

1. John 1:14 RSV.

Alexandria back in the fourth century, and I believe it. Word and flesh, flesh and Word. There in the dark of the Flint River as I stumbled along behind my friend, expecting to die, I thought about it what it meant. "The Word became what we are in order that we become what the Word is." Surely it is no less than this: "The Word became flesh that we might become Word."

"What has come into being in him was life, and the life was the light of all people. The light shines in the darkness, and the darkness did not overcome it."[2]

Light and Word. Back on the Flint River in that moment in the dark, my ankles wrapped around with blackberry stickers, the cold damp rising from the ground, my thirst crying out in my throat, and my whole body craving light, in that same moment, I looked up out of the corner of my eye and there in the sky, I saw a star.

2. John 1:3b-5 NRSV.

Chapter 5

The Darkness of God

A star. When I think now of that dark night I can hardly find the words to express what that star was, what that star meant to me. There is no doubt in my mind that it was a wonder—not that I mean by this that it was some utterly supernatural presence, some vision that never, apart from our immediate need, had hung on its own in the sky. It was natural, all right, a real star that shed its light, faint though it was, on real earth, a real river, real trees, and actual human beings.

But light in that darkness? I had given up hope of it long before, sometime after we had left the canoe. By now my need of light had transmuted itself from a mental, emotional hunger to a physical one, which, short of the undeniable urge to pick up my own crying baby and feed it, was as strong as any I had ever experienced. For hours as I stumbled along that unseen path my very body had longed for light, yearned for it, craved it more than my thirsty flesh yearned for water and my tired legs craved rest.

There is no way of knowing how much of the first glimmering of that star I missed, or even whether I missed any of it. I suspect that I didn't even notice it at first, squinting and concentrating as I was on my own interior jungle while I tried to read what had been written in the book of my life. Then, too, we had been walking almost the whole way through tall, thick brush under what could be called a canopy of trees only by the most far-fetched analogy. But perhaps I misspeak; it was a canopy, all right, one that hung in wet and dirty tatters over a sagging, dripping riverbed, a snake-draped hanging dense enough to provide a thick curtain between the night sky and our straining eyes.

I am not sure when I first took conscious notice of this star. Obviously, we would have had to have some visual access to the sky. This tells me that the three of us must have come out, at least for a little while, from under the overhanging foliage. Not that an absence of leaves and branches alone could have rendered that tiny spot of light visible; the cloud cover by now was so low it hung from the sky like wet laundry, wrapping itself around our bruised feet. The fact is, however, that a partial hole had to have opened at last in the thick air to let that star shine through.

In the beginning, it appeared to me only at the corner of my eye, a bright place at the side of my vision, so small and so faint that there was no way I could tell whether it was really there. Already fighting for escape, not only from the strangling darkness of the Flint River, but also from the underground places of my childhood nightmares in which I was buried alive, at first I could hardly believe that what I saw was not simply the product of my own wishful thinking. Hadn't my first husband, especially, warned me repeatedly that I ought never to trust the evidence of my own, unreliable senses? Perhaps, I thought, if my little spot of light were not the actual result of my craziness, it was only the simple product of some filthy, rotten matter that had crawled into and irritated my eye by means of a wet vine that a few minutes before had slapped me in the face.

What was that bright spot that had caught my attention? Was it my imagination? It worried me dreadfully that, when I turned my head and stared directly into the sky, it disappeared, yet when I looked away, miraculously, there it was again at the edge of my vision.

For a long time, I held my breath as I squinted and winked into the dark, not wanting to call Pam's and Jeff's attention to what I could not be sure was truly there. Then, at last, the faint glow brightened at the corner of my eye into a definite point of light. Dimmed by the clouds, and perhaps the distance as well, there was not much shine to it. Even so, as pale as phosphorescent moss, it was unmistakably a star: I could turn my head, look at it directly, and it would not disappear.

A star! I could hardly breathe. At that moment, it seemed to me, a star was all that I had ever wanted in life, all I could ever desire. It was my key to an inescapable closet, actual light in that dark place of dreams. A star! I lay down on it like a bed and drank it up like water. It was too dim to shed light to see by or to cast shadows. Still, that star spoke and shone into every molecule of my starving body, filling me, strengthening me, sustaining me. It was bread—the bread of life, bread made from wheat that had been scattered on the hillsides, brought together and ground to make a single, solid loaf, which fed me. It was light, and behind that light was God; and in that dreadful darkness, faint though it was, a single glimpse of it was milk and honey. It was surely enough to die by.

When I recall it now, I wonder over it still. What was the star we saw that night? Was it one of those praising stars from Psalm 19, a star that wandered randomly into our path, declaring the glory of God to anyone who would listen? Or was it, perhaps, a star more personal to me, one that had slipped away from its mates that night nearly thirty-five years earlier when I encountered the Word out by the dairy farm at Iowa State University? Or even more rationally improbable, and at the same time more likely to my heart, was this the star the Magi had seen in the East two thousand years before? Certainly, it was a particular star, and not a generic one, which led them straight to a barn at the end of their long trip, straight to a food trough in which a baby slept. It was a star, too, that persuaded them to leave their costly gifts in that unlikely place: gold for a king, incense for a god, myrrh for death.

With time, after all, twisting and turning, circling ever back upon itself the way it does in our actual lives, why could it not have been the Magi's star we saw that night, the star of the psalmist, the star of the cow barn, the Daystar from on high which dawned among us to shine on those who walked in darkness and in the shadow of death, to guide our feet in the way of peace?

Mulling over the nature of time and human participation in it has surely been a part of my ruminations on the identity of that star throughout the years. Not that I had not worried over it before. Indeed, though (to me, at least) I've been surprisingly uninterested in the future, I've pondered on time and memory and the nature of the past and present as long as I can remember. Certainly, the communion of the saints, life together in the eternal present of God, has been a mystery to me since I began to find myself continually confronted from one day to the next with the living presence of the ancient teachers I study. But it isn't only here in my professional and spiritual life I feel it. The common life I share with the long-dead women of my family on my mother's side is equally powerful and mysterious to me.

My friend Douglas and I had constant conversations on the nature of time back when we both were in high school; I remember him and those talks we had more frequently than I ever would have imagined when we were in our earlier years.

I met Douglas first when I was thirteen and a very young high school sophomore, through my boyfriend, Herbert, and his twin brother, Walter. During those years, under the benign supervision of their cultured parents, Herbert and Walter hung out with an odd, intelligent group of boys who had been Scouts together for a long time. Most of them were in our public school's orchestra; and some, like my twin friends, were also in the band, which was where, as a very bad flute player, I first got to know them. All of them were passionate about classical music. The first year I was allowed to be a regular part of their group, I recall, we were crazed with Dvorak's Slavonic Dances and Prokofiev's symphonies; the second year it was Bach and Mozart, especially the French horn concertos; and the third, it was operas, most particularly the big, heavy Russian ones.

We were a brainy group of half-children, half-adults then. We had a good time together on the weekends, going to concerts, movies at the University of Louisville or the local art theatres, or just sitting around, listening to the records we checked out of the public library and played on the Taylors' phonograph as we devoured pile after pile of muenster cheese and green olive sandwiches.

Apart from our common interests, there were other things my friends and I were concerned with, too. From the time I first knew him, Herbert intended to be an artist, and he filled his parents' well-lit, modern house with curving, floating mobiles of wire and balsa wood, as well as gas-powered model airplanes that really flew. Though they both liked literature, Walter and another of us, Jay, were scientifically inclined; Walter particularly was attracted to the complexities of abstract mathematical formulations. As for me, reading novels and reading and writing poetry as a means of making sense of my life were what I was drawn to do. Needless to say, because my own thoughts and feelings I was trying to understand and bring into order were so complex, the literature to which I was attracted was also complicated and multilayered: George Eliot, Dostoyevsky, Camus, Hopkins, the English metaphysical poets.

Apart from what I found in this literature, I never read

theological books. A high-minded, rationalistic, snobby bunch, none of us approved of religion. Having been reared with the values and prejudices of old-fashioned New England Unitarians, Herbert and Walter considered Christianity to be at best nothing more than self-deluding, self-serving emotionalism. Though I didn't approve of it either, I wasn't so sure where I was with religion, though I had sense enough to keep my mouth shut about my ambivalence. Certainly, my own preadolescent upbringing had included attendance at too many country Southern Baptist revivals for me to be able to write it off as simply wishful thinking—how could anybody in their right mind wish for what I heard there? Painful as all that talk of damnation was, I was too frightened by the possibilities inherent in it simply to write it off. At the same time, I was too attracted to the idea of a very different God I sometimes glimpsed at the edges of that talk.

In many ways Douglas was different from the other boys. It wasn't just that he appeared to attend a Presbyterian church regularly and happily with his mother and sister. He also hadn't been a Scout, and he didn't play a musical instrument; and this meant that he was in neither band nor orchestra with the rest of them. What really set him apart from the others, however, was his total lack both of interest and of talent in the hard sciences. Chemistry, physics, even biology—none began to suit him. This was serious. The fifties was a time, after all, when United States culture divided itself neatly and normatively into male and female. Men, of course, were meant to be the tough, abstract thinkers, the ones who favored science and its universal principles. Men understood the dangers of emotionalism, the unholy attraction to the particular at the expense of the universal. Women, on the other hand, were by definition inferior to men because they were irrational. They couldn't understand science and math because they were too emotional—bogged down, as they insisted on being, in the concrete, in the particular reality under their noses, in the physical, and even in the religious.

Douglas, who was clearly male, did not fit these normative and descriptive categories. Where his male friends were hard, Douglas was soft; where they were logical, he was dreamy; where they were organized, efficient, and full of energy, he was slow. Douglas liked to eat, and worst of all, he was "sensitive." He hated math and science (though he loved our chemistry teacher passionately). When he saw a child hurt, he cried; when he sniffed at roses, he closed his eyes with pleasure. He liked to quote romantic poetry as well as parts of *The Iliad* and *The Odyssey*. He was infinitely gentle and he never, ever bullied. With his dark floppy hair, long nose, delicate mouth, run-down loafers, and rumpled trousers from the pockets of which he never seemed to take his long-fingered, beautiful hands, he didn't even look like they looked.

The strangest thing of all, the most unmale thing about Douglas, however, was that he actually liked me. Now don't misunderstand me: the others liked me, too, but not in the way Douglas did. I think I was a kind of mascot for them; I'm not sure they ever took me seriously. They were fond of me, of course, in spite of my being an emotional, irrational girl; occasionally, though not often, I would impress them with some insight I had come up with or some arcane piece of knowledge I might produce. Certainly, they included me in most of their innings and their outings. Still, I don't believe they ever forgot for a minute that I was not only not like them, as a female I was a kind of mirror image of every way they didn't want to think, of everything they didn't want to be.

Douglas, however, didn't see me as they saw me. Unlike the rest of them, he never teased me about being female or pushed me to the point of tears. He had no interest in showing me up intellectually or demonstrating his male superiority. To him, I was a girl, yes, a girl to whom he was attracted. More important, however, I was a person whose company he enjoyed, a kindred soul who understood him when he talked about the things that really interested him. After all, I, too, was almost helplessly fascinated with the convoluted mental puzzles that delighted yet plagued and even tortured him. We were two children lost in a world in which we could not find a place, and it was a relief to wonder together over the nature of reality, of human consciousness and death, and intertwined with everything else, the baffling nature of time.

A skinny, anxious fifteen-year-old girl and a melancholy, odd-looking sixteen-year-old boy walking after school through the rough grass between the tall trees of Cherokee Park, we talked endlessly, almost obsessively, of these things.

When I've thought of Douglas over the years, I've often remembered a conversation we had one day on what it meant to die, which in some ways was our most confusing problem of all, considering how, for us, time, consciousness, and the nature of reality were all jumbled up in it together. On this day even more than usual, I was worried that there was something wrong with me for wondering about these things, but I couldn't seem to keep away from the guilty pleasure of being able to discuss them with another human being.

"Douglas," I remember saying that afternoon, "for the life of me, I can't understand death at all. It just doesn't make sense."

"In what way doesn't it make sense?" Douglas responded. "I don't have any trouble with it; if a person has a beginning, then he will have to have an end. Of course he dies."

"No, no, the problem isn't that," I said, not entirely truthfully. I had a really hard time with the notion that a person could actually over the period of a year go from being nothing to having at least as much consciousness as a baby has.

"Doesn't it seem to you that nothing that happens to human beings actually becomes real until they recall it later, even if it is only a minute or two later? It certainly seems that way to me." I was still young enough to think that unless a person could take her conscious experience and, through the exercise of memory, organize it into some kind of story later, even if it were only a moment later, then that original experience didn't count as "real."

"Well, yes, of course," said Douglas, frowning. "I believe that, but I don't understand what this has to do with dying."

"Well, let me think how to say it," I replied, aware of

my gratitude. No one else would have ever let me talk about these things without accusing me of craziness or at least emotionalism; I wouldn't have tried to have this conversation with anyone in the world except Douglas.

It was a wet hot day in late spring; without my noticing, the sky darkened slowly over the pale green treetops as I considered my answer. I tried to focus on the idea with which I was struggling. I jumped a little when lightning flashed in the gray air; a little while later thunder rolled over it softly.

"Try this one out," I said at last. "If something that happens to us only becomes real to us when we remember it later and think about what it means, then how can dying be possible? After all, the very fact of being dead makes it impossible for us to remember dying, doesn't it?"

I could see immediately that to Douglas, an adolescent like me whose life largely consisted of mulling over every event and emotion that came to him, what I said made perfect sense. As I waited for his response, I watched as he nodded his head and stuck his hands even deeper in his pockets.

"Yes," he said, picking up my thought, "but there are other things we can't remember, too, that we know actually do happen, like being born. Nobody remembers being born, and who is to say what a baby thinks while it's going on? I'm not even sure babies think."

He had a point, and his point made me consider something else. "What happens," I wondered, "when a person is in a car wreck and right afterward she tells someone else about it, but she can't remember any of it later? If it isn't in her memory, then where is it? It obviously happened, but if she couldn't remember it the next day, was she really conscious when she described it the day before? Can you be conscious but have no memory of it later?"

Douglas frowned and thought about it.

Now, at this point we might have turned our talk to a logical discussion of moral responsibility in cases of insanity, but we didn't. Though morality was also an endlessly fascinating topic to the two of us, it wasn't at all what we were interested in here, but rather what it meant to be self-aware in such a way that self-awareness was manifested in being able to make sense of the things around us. And, of course, as abstract as all this sounded, it wasn't simply theoretical to either of us. We were wondering where, in some literal sense, the two of us began and where we ended, and how we were affected by our beginnings and endings.

By now we were sitting shoulder to shoulder in the grass on the wet ground as we leaned back against the trunk of a large maple tree that was dressed for our pleasure in its new, light green leaves. Becoming aware of each other's bodies in a pleasant sort of way that neither of us was about to acknowledge, we were quiet for a minute as we tried to sort out what seemed to us both to be psychologically and even physically impossible.

After a while I said tentatively, "Maybe all this has something to do with the way time works."

Douglas turned to face me, idly taking one of my hands. I made use of my other hand to pick an ant off my disheveled pleated skirt and to smooth down my pony tail.

"What do you mean?" he asked.

Again, I tried to find the words that would enable me to drag in what I was trying to get hold of at the very edges of my consciousness. "Did it ever occur to you to think that things might not take place one after the other the way they seem to? Maybe they actually all happen at once, and we human beings just have to sort them out into *before* and *after* to make sense of them.

"I'll tell you what," I went on. "I already know time is not something that is fixed; how we perceive it varies from person to person. I know it is different for children than it is for us. I remember how long a week was when I was in kindergarten, longer than a month is now. What do you think time feels like to an amoeba or to an elephant or," I said, picking one out of the air that was hovering around my nose, "to a gnat?"

I hesitated before I went on because I couldn't imagine how he would answer me. "How do you think time looks to God?"

Douglas thought about all this for a while. When he responded, he avoided the question of God altogether. "If time weren't fixed, it would certainly explain a lot," he said.

I didn't press the point; I knew it was as far as we could go in that conversation. Simultaneously, we stood up; we faced each other and smiled, satisfied with the forbidden boundaries we had crossed together.

Two years later Douglas went on to college out of state, and a year after that, I went away myself. For whatever reason, we weren't able to write to each other much while I was a freshman, and we hardly ever saw each other, even when we were both at home. There was a flowery, melodramatic letter that he sent to me while he was a sophomore. In it he described his discovery of wine at a fraternity party and what he considered to be the pleasures of drunkenness. I worried about what was happening to him, though not as much as I would today, considering what I know now about alcoholism.

After my marriage the following summer, I had no contact with him for many years. At my brother's wedding more than twenty years ago, I'll admit I suffered a jealous twinge when I learned that he was working for a magazine in Manhattan and dating the girl friend of my new sister-in-law. Ten years or so later my mother wrote to tell me that Douglas was dead. Still working at the magazine, he had been dating someone else by now. He had taken a vacation in Mexico; I imagine him alone, but I don't really know that this was the case. At any rate, he contracted spinal meningitis there. Apparently self-diagnosing it as a cold, he died a few days after he returned.

Though there had been a time when he and I had shared our secrets, wrestling together over what were to us the most intimate facts of the universe, it had been so long since I had seen him that we had become strangers. What he thought about in his final hours I can't imagine, but even if he had not been very ill, I don't believe it would have been our long ago conversation about death and time. It is very hard for me to think about him as the loving, lonely teenager he was, dying by himself.

It doesn't strike me as very likely that I will ever learn more of Douglas's years in New York now, much less of the last hours of his life. Still, I try to hold my memories of him—or rather, him, himself, really—in the same two hands that smoothed down my skirt and hair under the tree in the park all those years ago. Age-spotted as these hands are, there is something in the physical continuity of my present body with my past, and my past body with his, even in their accidental touching, that does not let him die entirely.

Of course, it had been the nature of self-consciousness that we had puzzled over, and not our bodies, which had been hardly more than an embarrassment to us. At fifteen and sixteen, neither Douglas nor I could conceive of the human in other terms. The older I get, however, the more I understand the longing not just to read the words, but to love and touch the very bones of the saints. I suppose the insistence on a physical, bodily connection to the dead is a refusal to accept the discontinuity of time; it is a denial of the power of mortality in the face of love.

This, then, is Douglas's life as I hold it as best I can, both physically and in memory, but, of course, there is more to his life than this because I am not its only holder. Whatever I thought in high school, I cannot help believing now that, in the eternal memory of God, Douglas is preserved alive and whole, as we Christians say, "unto everlasting life." How this can be, in a literally mechanical sense, I do not know, nor does it worry me. Perhaps I've mentioned before, however, how happy I was to learn that many of the early Christians who are my own teachers were convinced that, just as the two of us speculated so many years ago, in the mind of God all things exist simultaneously.

Does what I believe about Douglas, about the continuity of human bodies through touch and the persistence of human life in the mind of God, sound crazy? It is no crazier than the claim of the early church—out of which my convictions come that in the person of Jesus, God the Word in whose image every human being is made, became flesh—that God, out of love for mortal human beings, took human flesh, soul, heart, as God's very own. Nor is it odder than the idea that God—not some poor helpless human victim made to suffer by a just God, but God, God's own self—took the flesh of all of us to die in it and thereby defeat death. Is what I believe about Douglas crazier than the thought that in the incarnation, because God took them as God's very own, our poor suffering bodies and minds are both deeply honored and preserved even as they are drawn out of death into the life and light of God?

But the thought of the light of God brings me back once more to the Flint River and that star which so surprisingly appeared in its hanging darkness. From the beginning the appearance of the star has brought me again and again to mull over the meaning of the paradox that came with it: why it should be true that, while the star never literally shone much light into that wilderness that night, it was and still is enough for me to die by.

It was such a small, pale brilliance, after all; it wasn't even visible for very long, quickly covered over again as it was by the heavy clouds and the dripping boughs above us. Yet, by the time it faded, as it did so quickly, it had already given me what I needed. It led me out of the place I had been so that I could walk once more blind into the thick darkness, this time, however, not as into the tomb I had fought against in my childhood dreams but into the utter mystery of the Word who is also the unknowable, ungraspable, unnameable, and unspeakable God.

Not that the fading of the star and my re-entry into the darkness of God brought me at once to some high, noble, mystical moment; what happened was much more mundane than that. I was sorry to lose sight of the friendly and immediately familiar light, to be sure; at the same time I was surprised to notice that I was not truly grieved by its loss. Having tasted it, drunk it, and lain down on it, I had been satisfied by it, soul and body, yet I could also be perfectly happy to let go of it and, along with it, of all that it had, interiorly at least, shone its light upon, even my own life. Why this should have been the case was once a puzzle to me; now, I think I understand it.

In the sixth century, Dorotheos of Gaza delivered a homily to the monks of his monastery on renunciation, which he speaks of as coming to the point where a person is able to give up all "extraneous desires." This cutting off of desire, as he describes it, results from a process of giving up "self-will" little by little so that the monk's "passionate attachment" to the world is broken. This is a very unmodern process.

> A man takes a little walk and sees something, [Dorotheos tells his listeners]. His thoughts say to him, "Go over there and investigate," and he says to his thoughts, "No! I won't," and he cuts off his desire. Again, he finds someone gossiping, and his thoughts say to him, "You go and

have a word with them," and he cuts off his desire and does not speak. . . . [At last, a] man denying himself in this way comes little by little to form a habit of it, so that from denying himself in little things, he begins to deny himself in great without the least trouble. . . .[1]

As Dorotheos speaks of it, then, the process of renunciation involves letting go of the distracting, grasping, and controlling aspects of imagination.

But even so, why should anyone want to give up the imagination, much less everything else that has to be given up with it? And what sense, particularly, could it be given up by a woman reared to believe that her whole moral life should be about setting aside all of her own needs and longings for the sake of satisfying the desires, even whims, of her family? I couldn't accept Dorotheos's renunciation as a modern virtue at all. Without looking at it more closely, I had to relegate it to the same place in which I put the early monastic attempt to function on the least sleep, food, and water possible: it was from another culture, another age, and not really possible or even relevant in our own.

After the night on the Flint River, after what happened with the disappearance of the star, I think I understand renunciation a little better. Certainly, as Dorotheos later goes on to speak of it, it has very little to do with that put-upon woman whose virtue, in a manner of speaking, comes from her long-suffering in the face of her husband

1. *Dorotheos of Gaza, Discourses and Sayings*, trans. Eric P. Wheeler (Kalamazoo, Mich: Cistercian Publications, 1977), p. 91.

and children's ill treatment of her. Indeed, the point of such renunciation in the monastic life is the very opposite of being miserable. As Dorotheos says, having cut off desires one at a time:

> [The monk] finally . . . comes not to have any of these extraneous desires, but whatever happens to him he is satisfied with it, as if it were the very thing he wanted. And so, not desiring to satisfy his own desires, he finds himself always doing what he wants to. For not having his own special fancies, he fancies every single thing that happens to him.[2]

Once more, we are in a paradox. The monk renounces everything, even his own desires, not because it is morally wrong to desire, but so that he can receive everything that happens to him with happiness, fully attentive to what actually is.

But the desire to control "everything that happens" to a person is not all that some of the ancient teachers recommend giving up in order to be able to arrive at an encounter with what is. For Pseudo-Dionysius, a representative of Christian Platonism and roughly a sixth-century contemporary of Dorotheos, a fundamental kind of renunciation is also necessary if we are to enter into one of the two basic ways we human beings have of knowing God.

In the first way about which this tradition speaks, we come to know God through what we are able to describe

2. Ibid., pp. 88-89.

as we make use of human words and concepts. For example, we are able to come to know God as being, life, kindness, as Father, Son, and Holy Spirit, as just, slow to anger, good, true, and beautiful. These "positive" qualities of God are the things we read about God in scripture, are taught by our tradition, and even experience of God for ourselves. Here, the process of learning and knowing God is the result of a kind of gathering in, of "acquiring" more and more.

In the second way of knowing God, however, we come to God, not in terms we can describe, but with an acute awareness of the truth that God does not even begin to fit our human descriptions and categories. This tradition of the early church is clarified by its use of an image from scripture: when Moses requested to see God's glory at Mount Sinai, God refused, saying, "You cannot see my face and live." At the same time, however, God promised to put Moses in the cleft of a rock, covering it until God went by, then removing the cover so that Moses could see God's "backsides." What knowledge, therefore, did Moses gain of God from this cleft? It was the knowledge of God in the "divine darkness." This kind of knowing is described as negative knowing, a "knowing by not-knowing," a deep, paradoxical gut-understanding that while it is true that God really is Life, for example, and Goodness, as we encounter God in the created world, God is also not alive or good in the same way human or any other created beings are, because God is beyond any human categories, beyond everything we would define as life or goodness or anything else recognizably created. According to Dionysius, we reach this deep personal knowledge of God not by reasoning our way to it, but by another process of renunciation, a renunciation of all our ordinary ways of using our senses and intellectual abilities as we give ourselves up to the "being-beyond-being" of God.

Dionysius, as he speaks from this tradition, might sound very esoteric, very unconnected to the experience of a star and its absence on the Flint River more than fourteen hundred years later; but in fact, when I try now to make sense and learn of God from that night, I believe there is really not very much esoteric in it. With respect to God, after all, none of this "knowing God in the darkness," this knowing by not-knowing, was ever meant to be a mere intellectual exercise. It was always the case, I think, that a person who sought this knowledge was also seeking an intimate and real sense of connection with God's own unapproachable self. At the same time, however, and at least as important, the one who practiced this way of knowing God by not knowing was also practicing not just a certain way of being with God but also a way of being fully present with real people in the everyday experience of the reality human beings live in.

It is the case that when we try truly to know any other human beings, we must come to know them in both these positive and negative ways at once, just as we know God. Human beings, because we are made in the image of God, after all, are no more reducible to the facts of our lives and the things that can be said about us than God is. We can and must speak accurately about ourselves and one another in terms of our place of birth, our rearing, our present work, our appearance, our patterns of behavior, our temperament, and so forth. All this is "positive knowledge," as they used to say. It is real, and it is very important.

At the same time, all real knowledge, all real love depends on our equal understanding that not one of us can ever truly know someone else definitively. I can never say "I know Mary," for example, "as well as I know myself." As well as I may know her, I will never see the world through her eyes or experience her memories and hopes as she does. This is not just because I don't have enough information, either, enough "facts." Even if Mary is my child, conceived and carried in my own body and raised in my own household, Mary is other than I, not an extension of myself, and I will never fully share in that irreducible bit of life that makes her not-me, no matter how much I try to push aside or deny her otherness from me. Indeed, if I am truly to know her and so to love her, I must know her both positively, "in the light," and unknowingly, negatively, "in the darkness." A serious argument against capital punishment, not to mention the judgmentalism we are all prone to in everyday life, is it not?

And that brings me back both to Douglas and to the questions Douglas and I used to wrestle with as we tried—unsuccessfully, we thought—to make sense of human self-consciousness, time, and mortality. About our questions, I no longer believe that our attempts to grasp these things were unsuccessful. What we were engaged in, after all, was very much the kind of process of learning by standing outside the self or by the renunciation of the ordinary sensual and intellectual activities that I have just been speaking of. Of course we could never seize hold of death with our minds because we could never reduce either human self-consciousness or time to something we could grasp. Still, we did come right up to the alien, irreducible human and divine mystery we sought to understand, and we knew it, indeed, by our unknowing. I was touched by that mystery, too, in some permanent way.

As for Douglas himself, when I heard of his death so many years before, I was almost sick with grief. How could I bear it that the first real friend of my early adult life, this man who had once been as close to me as my own breath, was dead? As it had seemed to the two of us once long ago, death itself, the snuffing out of Douglas's consciousness, struck me as impossible. Now, though he had rarely occupied my mind in the preceding years, I thought of Douglas continuously. I woke up in the night with the shape of his nose and mouth before my eyes, the texture of his teenaged skin. Phrases of his—indeed, whole conversations—came to me unbidden, as did the sound of his laughter. Douglas was gone into that place we had struggled to make sense of, the place where there was no remembering, and I could neither understand it nor bear it.

Over the years the pain of loss faded, but it was only a lessening of pain, not a change in kind. That night on the Flint River, however, after the star disappeared and I truly found myself in the darkness of God, that change mysteriously began to take place. The change was the gift of renunciation.

I've already mentioned my surprise at finding how easy it was to give up that star I'd so hungered for, how willing I was to have been satisfied with what I'd received from it and then to let it go. I do not believe I've said, however, that along with the disappearance of the star and its light, I found myself all of a sudden in a state of being very like the one I believe that Dorotheos describes as renunciation. Whereas until that moment, my relationship with God, my family, my friends, my life and my impending death, my losses, my work, and everything else I had always valued had filled my consciousness and I had held them with gratitude, now I was emptied of all active thought, feeling, evaluation, and intention.

Oddly, paradoxically, though I expected more than ever that I would soon die, my emptiness had nothing in it of the hollowness of despair. It wasn't even resignation. Rather, it was, as Dorotheos says, a positive thing, a kind of "fancying of everything" that was happening to me in spite of what it was. And with this "fancying of everything" came a sense of being in the presence of the God I had come over the last few years to know, a God whose love was utterly trustworthy, even God the Word who made all things, keeps all things, and re-creates all things. Yet, at the same time, I knew that I didn't know this God at all. Trustworthy and loving, yes, revealed by the Word in Jesus Christ, infinitely lovable, attractive, delightful, but God and the things of God, time, consciousness, death, were also so utterly beyond my grasp, so unkowable to my knowing, that I could not conceive of them, much less sum them up. This was fine with me.

Out of the gift of this renunciation I gave up Douglas and my beloved dead: my father, my aunt, my grandmother and my great-aunts, Stephan, my ancient teachers, and my modern teachers, too, who have died; I gave up all of them to the good and generous God of life and love I know like my own hands and feet, who is also totally beyond my knowing. God holds these dead in life, as God holds us all. I believe God holds them in consciousness and in body, too, though what consciousness and body can mean in this time beyond time I wouldn't presume to say, only that it is in the communion of the saints, the kingdom of heaven which is the garden of paradise, the New Jerusalem.

Where did my blessed renunciation come from that long night? Surely, it wasn't, as both Dorotheos and Dionysius would have insisted it must be, from my own ascetic and intellectual discipline. Indeed, I am not sure that under the normal circumstances of life in the modern world it is even possible to train oneself to the point of being able to "fancy everything that happens." Even if it is, it seems well nigh impossible to discipline oneself utterly to renounce the ordinary ways of perception and thought. Still, God never leaves any of us without the thing we most need, which is God's own self. For this reason, renunciation was given to me that night when the star faded as a gift of God's grace.

And thus, on the Flint River, after the star had closed its eye, after I had received the whole of what it had to give, at least for a little while I renounced everything. I walked on in the presence of the known and unknown God through the good darkness between my two friends, also known and unknown, through time, through mud and wet leaves, sticking vines and slapping branches. Cold, hungry, and very thirsty, I was content to die.

Chapter 6

Another Light

I t was a long time that we went on like this, much
longer than any of us realized until later, but that is
the way time was that night, as impossible to gauge
as the distance between an up-raised foot and the
invisible ground. We warmed up a little; at least Pam and
I did. As we walked our wet clothes began to dry, stiff on
our bodies. Though thirst is harder to drive away than
hunger, my stomach had stopped growling much earlier
and my imagination had cut off its supply of the images,
smells, and textures of crisp, hot French fries and softly
stringy pork barbecue, glistening with grease and
drenched in a red vinegar sauce, which I'd eaten for
lunch with my friends not long before we saw the
gnawed-on deer carcass at the put-in point of the river.

I didn't know what Pam was thinking through these
last hours, for none of us felt the urge to talk. I was certain, however, that she didn't want me to ask her and so
put her in a position where she might have to examine
her feelings or her judgment and come upon some serious doubts about our situation that might demoralize her

and us. As far as I could tell, as the unofficial leader of our expedition she was still completely alert and totally present. Her spirits and her energy appeared to have remained high in spite of our continuing inability to recognize where we were, and neither her cheerfulness nor her affectionate kindness showed any signs of faltering.

I had no idea what was going on in Jeff's head in the way of thoughts, or whether his or Pam's interior considerations, experiences, and prayer, for that matter, bore much resemblance to my own. I assumed that the pain in his knee had become worse as the night passed. In his thin T-shirt and shorts, he continued to have to stagger along on it in the chill air, propping himself up on his wooden paddle and further twisting the torn cartilage and ligaments of his leg as he stepped into root-filled holes and splashed through sandy-bottomed streams. I was almost certain that he managed his suffering by a kind of concentration that allowed him to build an enormous internal wall against letting himself feel it fully. I would certainly no more have asked him what he was thinking or how he felt than I would have asked Pam; I suspected that any attempt on his part to talk with us would drag him back up from wherever he was inside himself and break both his concentration and his ability to control the pain.

Whatever was going on in Pam's and Jeff's heads, neither was overtly in need of anything from me beyond what I had already given; and neither of them, to my knowledge, was afraid. I was grateful that I was left, therefore, to continue on into this known and unknown darkness in the way I was already going. Occasionally, I thought of the canoe tied up to a fallen tree somewhere behind us, and I wondered if it would sit there forever or pull loose and float off in the spring floods. Would the boat be found by children playing by the water miles downstream, and if it were, would their parents look in vain for me, its owner? Perhaps it would only be found by the hunters whose shotguns we could still hear, but if it were, what would they think had happened to us?

I didn't really worry about the canoe or anything else, for that matter. In the aftermath of the star and its renunciation I was at peace. Though this peace failed to modulate the physical darkness into something less than impenetrable, or smooth out the terrain I walked through, I was strangely content.

And so Pam, Jeff, and I walked on together slowly, carefully, perhaps two hours, perhaps many more. The bird calls dropped off, as well as the soft rustling of small animals in the undergrowth. With them, the comforting swish and whisper of automobile tires on distant asphalt faded from my ears. In the silence, occasionally we stopped to rest on a log or lean against a tree, Pam and I huddled together. Considering the state we were all in by now, it was only the double danger of the hypothermia that faced the lot of us and the threat of Jeff's knee freezing up that kept us from stopping more often. Every now and then one of us would step a few feet off the invisible path to relieve ourselves, as we had been doing since the sun had set; from the beginning, the darkness was so thick that the danger of becoming separated from our companions was more serious than the need for privacy.

What finally jerked me up from the interior place I had

been and brought me back to speech was the glow of an electric light. I didn't understand what I was looking at when I first saw it gleaming low and yellow, hanging in the trees like a tiny lantern. Still, unlike the actual star, which had had to materialize in the corner of my eye before it was truly visible, teasing me with its ethereal "now but not yet" quality, it was obvious that this light was no product of my imagination.

Small though it was, from the minute I saw it, I knew it was a light of human origin. Without hesitation my avaricious imagination seized hold of it and mounted it over the front porch of a large, rustic but comfortable one-story cabin that sat on the bank of the river. Met in my own story by a tail-wagging, jumping dog, in a few minutes I expected us to tramp up the front steps of the cabin, shake the mud and leaves off our filthy clothing, and knock on its door. An elderly man and woman would open it together, fuss over us, and invite us in. After encouraging me to call Richard to tell him that in spite of everything I was alive, they would set us down in the living room in comfortable chairs which had already been covered with old towels to protect them from our dirt.

Then, while we rested our tired feet on the beautiful handmade braided rug and warmed ourselves at the enormous fire they would have built for us in the stone fireplace, we would quench our thirst with all the water we could hold and fill our stomachs with fragrant fried chicken, mashed potatoes and gravy, greens, and biscuits which had been prepared for a family reunion the next day. Though our hosts would urge us to spend the night, of course they would understand our longing for home.

Thus sated and happy, we would be loaded into their car and driven far down the road to our waiting van, all the time exclaiming on the luck that had brought us to their door.

"Pam! Jeff!" At the very thought of all this, I called in excitement to my friends. "Look, it's an electric light; we must be close to a house!"

"Do you see it, Pam?" I cried out again when no one answered. "What do you think it is?" More cautious in my speech than in my imagination, I kept the details of my fantasy to myself.

In the dark I heard Pam somewhere in front of me trudging back to where I had stopped. She leaned against the trunk of a slippery tree I was standing by to look for herself. "You're right," she said at last. "I see it. I'm almost sure it's not a house, though; I think it's the light on the bridge that is supposed to cross the river. It's good news if it is."

"Bridge?" I answered her. I was stupefied by the idea that we might find a way to escape and I might not actually die. This was the first I had heard that we should have been looking for a bridge. "What makes you say that?"

"Why, it was clearly marked on the map we studied before we ever left the car," she replied, amazed at my previous ignorance of its existence. "We had to be able to recognize the landmarks along our way. Didn't you think of it?"

Not being either a wilderness hiker or a map reader, in fact I hadn't thought of it. Furthermore, wherever the light was coming from, no bridge was visible to me.

Indeed, I wasn't even sure I believed in its existence. It struck me that the condition of the river, after all, had turned out to be utterly unlike its description in the book Pam had. Why should a map be right? Besides, I was reluctant to give up my vision of a welcoming porch, a telephone, and a hot meal, no matter how unlikely it was.

"Yes, but Pam," I answered cautiously, "don't you think it could be a house we're seeing? Look how low the light is. It's too yellow to be an arc light." Perhaps it wasn't a house or a bridge, but I was sure what I saw was real, and the bulb had to be hanging from something.

Whatever it was, bridge or something else, I tried to swallow down the hope that was rising in my throat. Under the circumstances, surely that hope ought not to be trusted. Even if it were, however, it was making me feel my tiredness. To beat back my own optimism I said to her tentatively, "It could be a barn, you know, Pam. It doesn't have to be a place where people live."

Unexpectedly, Jeff voice's cut in from somewhere behind me. "It's not a barn; it's the bridge, all right." He had been silent till now; I hadn't realized Jeff had even heard us. I was so surprised, it jolted me again.

"It *is* the bridge," Pam replied in the special tone of voice my friend uses when she is certain of something and also very pleased with herself. "I know it's the bridge. We'll be there soon."

Whether it was or not, her words were enough to drag me out of the temporary insanity I had fallen into over the imaginary house. Sanity brought its own problems. "I wonder what time it is," I answered, anxiously now. I was no longer able to close my eyes to my painfully trustworthy images of Richard wandering restlessly through the house, wondering whether we were dead by now, and if we weren't, what terrible things were happening to us.

"It's early. I don't think it's midnight yet," Jeff answered. It suited me to think him right.

Pam didn't say anything; she had already picked up her paddle and gathered herself together to continue walking.

Oddly, for me, the following hours, when the electric light was visible but not attainable, were the hardest of the night and certainly the most endless. For one thing, the three of us had been convinced when we first saw it that whatever the light before us was, we were almost to it; yet we walked and walked without its ever seeming to get closer. There was a logical reason for it, of course. Even if we already knew it, none of us was inclined to remember how far away a human eye can be from the smallest candle flame before its flickering disappears into the swallowing darkness. Each of us had certainly forgotten the actual light years, the millions upon millions of miles, that separated the light of the star which had earlier appeared to us from our hungry earthbound sight.

Then, too, it had been hours since we had looked at our watches, and we had had no way to mark the passage of time since night had fallen. Having long since accustomed ourselves to the barely moving pace at which we dragged and pushed ourselves with paddles through the dark, we didn't realize how terribly slowly we were traveling. This meant, however, that we were not able to measure time subconsciously as we all ordinarily do by how long it took us to walk a certain distance.

Mostly, however, when I think about it now, it seems that for me, at least, the painfulness of those last hours was a direct result of my total abandonment of my recently acquired ability to renounce myself and my life which had been given to me as a gift when the light of the star faded into the sky. It wasn't an accident, after all, that this new loss came simultaneously both with the sight of a human light and the recurrence of a whole set of specific and insistent desires, including a strong desire to live. I remember very well, after all, a story included in the *Sayings of the Fathers.*

There was once a monk named Apphy from the south of Egypt who was made a bishop, very likely under actual duress, as was often the case in the exuberant life of the early church. Whether he wanted the job or had been forced into it, however, Apphy was determined to deal with it by continuing his monastic disciplines as he served the church away from the desert. This he tried very hard to do. He could not understand it, however, when he discovered that no matter how hard he tried,

he had not the strength to do so. Therefore he prostrated himself before God saying, "Has your grace left me because of my episcopate?" Then, he was given this revelation, "No, but when you were in solitude and there was no one else it was God who was your helper. Now that you are in the world, it is [human beings]."[1]

1. Apphy 1, *Sayings,* p. 35.

In the distant, empty desert, when there had been nothing else for Apphy to do and no one else to comfort him or help him, having renounced all else, it was God upon whom he had thrown himself, God who had been the lens through which he had seen everything, thought of everything, and done everything. Once having rejoined the world, however, even for the best and most innocent of reasons, he could not but live in the world according to its own terms.

Even on its best terms, values, expectations, and hopes, which in his case would surely have been Christian ones, Apphy's life could never again be the same for him as it had been when he had given up everything in exchange for God. There was nothing wrong with being a bishop. It was only that in the desert where his heart was at peace because he fancied every single thing that came to him, stretching out before him for the whole of his life and into his death, there was only God, the love of God, and the love of neighbor. Now, he was once more in the world where bishops fought with other bishops, negotiated with the government on behalf of the people of their villages, supervised the clergy, and exercised pastoral care over their congregations.

I should not have been surprised, therefore, that the last hours on the Flint River were my hardest. Unlike that of the monks of the desert, renunciation had not come to me as a result of my own discipline. I had been given the gift of renunciation only for a little while so that I, too, could walk, as I believed, toward my own death, paying intense attention to what was around me, fancying everything, waiting on everything known and unknown, seeing and not seeing God. With the sight of the human light, the visual symbol of my familiar life, I renounced my renunciation. Now, to my sorrow, I found myself full of very specific controlling hungers, needs, and cravings—first of all, for Richard, for his peace of mind and his love, but also for safety, for food and water, for sleep in my own bed, for a dry, clean body, for far more light, for my home, my family, my students, and my friends. All of these desires were legitimate and good. Their goodness and legitimacy, however, did not prevent my being nearly consumed by attention to what was going on in my own body that I could not prevent: my legs ached, my back hurt, and my tongue seemed as dry and cracked as dirty leather.

As for God and what I'd learned of God in this wilderness, believe me, God was not forgotten. Though the extraordinary, unknown presence of God was gone for now from my immediate experience, it would be there to revisit for pondering, as it always is, again and again over the years. The beloved, intimate, ordinary presence of God was still there, holding up the ground, providing the light and the darkness, letting me feel the hunger and the thirst, comforting and strengthening my heart, and sustaining hope. And there, too, in the person of Pam, known to me like a sister and yet unknown, was God's own self.

From the moment when Pam connected the light with the bridge, the urge to go faster than we had been going was almost unbearable. Relying on her paddle to keep her balance and knock away offending spiderwebs and other unspeakable things, Pam positively strode (relatively speaking) into the jungly darkness of underbrush and branches. Under the impetus of the distant light, she discovered that the faint animal trail we had been following along the edge of the river had suddenly become more visible. We were all re-energized. Behind me, Jeff silently crashed on, though I sensed that his focus had shifted from inner to outer and his mood was changing.

Whatever was going on with Pam and Jeff, my own mood was strangely divided. On the one hand, in my soggy sweatpants, raincoat, and muddy, sticky shoes, I slopped along as fast as I could between my two friends like a clumsy but enthusiastic wet dog. Though I tried my best to concentrate on where I put my feet, I tripped over roots and fell into holes, pulled myself up with my paddle, fell and pulled myself up again. On the other hand, from the time night had descended many hours before, I had hardly felt the hurt of my injuries; now, in the very sight of home, each fall seemed to compound my bruises, multiply my aches, and demoralize me. Suddenly, my hunger became far more insistent, and I was so thirsty I was nearly ready to drink the dirty water of the river below us.

Hunger and thirst, however, were not soon to be satisfied. We walked and stumbled, fell and tripped along as fast as we could, but it was some time before we began to realize that however we hurried, we didn't seem to be getting closer to the bridge. For what seemed like hours and may actually have been so, the yellow light receded in front of us, winking and bobbing through the trees at exactly the pace we walked. However we tried to trick ourselves and it, when we stopped, it stopped; when we started up again, it did, too. Whatever Pam and Jeff were feeling by this time, I didn't want to ask; but now, once help was both in sight and out of reach, I came close to despairing.

I think it was only after a very small act of renunciation—my first deliberate one of the evening when I gave up, stopped longing for the bridge and merely began to watch for it—that I was able to notice that the woods through which we walked seemed to be changing. The ground became smooth and gritty with sand under our feet, and there were fewer branches and blackberry stickers slapping our faces and catching our legs. All at once, the light grew brighter and higher in the sky, and we could see what it was we were moving toward. It was, indeed, the bridge, and it stretched out in the indeterminate distance before us, solidly, grayly, and beautifully illumined by the tall highway light that arced over it.

"Do you see it?" I called out to my friends in excitement. Renunciation had been renounced again.

"I do," Pam shouted back to me.

"Yup!" said laconic Jeff from behind.

The three of us had slowed down spontaneously, and I was impatient. "Let's not stop now," I said.

"That's okay with me," said Pam. "Let's keep going."

Our attention entirely focused on our destination, the three of us walked on now more quickly than ever. Where before our sight had been drawn to the light in front of us, now it was positively fixed in place. The shape of the bridge drifted in and out of our field of vision, then the illuminated sky above it, the road running over it, and the concrete pillars holding it up out of the dark water in which the overhead light was so perfectly reflected. Finally, the long, steep, grassy approach to it symmetrically appeared, panoramically stretching out neatly in front of our path to the left and right.

When the whole of it rose up before us in its full glory, we were positively mesmerized with relief and happiness. Chins in the air and cricks in our necks, for a long time we simply stood where we were, gazing at it with our mouths hanging open.

It was Pam who shook herself at last, wrenched her eyes away from the bridge, and set down her pack beside her. Looking around us for the first time, suddenly she saw where we had actually landed ourselves.

"Oh, no!" she exclaimed. "Bobbie, Jeff, look down," she said. "I can't believe it!"

Suddenly dry-mouthed from thirst and anxiety, Jeff and I lowered our eyes to the sight in front of us.

"Oh, no!" I am sorry to report I wailed ignominiously when I saw it. "I can't stand it! I just can't stand it!"

At the same time, Jeff started laughing. "Well, look what we did," he said over my wailing. Surprised, I shut up and looked at him. For the first time in hours I could see the shape of him; he was shaking his head as he leaned on his paddle in the sand, as he kept on laughing. Pretty soon Pam joined in, and I did, too.

"Just look at that!" Pam said, gasping. She pointed to the water that stretched out absolutely impassable between us and the edifice before us. "We were so busy keeping our eyes on the bridge that we walked right out onto a spit in the river."

Sure enough, that was what we had done. It was no wonder the ground had turned sandy under our feet and the foliage disappeared. No wonder the bridge extended itself before us so symmetrically to our right and left as we walked. Even if there hadn't been water between ourselves and it, everyone knows that there is no way to climb onto a bridge if you are standing directly under it.

At last the laughter died away at the ridiculousness of our position. We pulled ourselves together, picked up our stuff, and prepared to face the inevitable.

"Okay," said Pam, our leader still. "We're going to have to turn around and follow the bank back until we can find a place that looks like we can ford it."

I closed my eyes and swallowed two or three times. Perhaps I made a sound in my throat, because she came over to me and put her arms around me then. "Are you all right, Bobbie Marie?" she asked. "It's just a little farther; you can make it, now."

Just hearing her say it put me back on my worn-out feet. Once more I was flooded with gratitude to Pam for being Pam, for her goodness, cheerfulness, and energy, as well as her quietness and her refusal to let herself be irritable or blaming. No matter how bad things had become, it was these qualities in her that I had rested in all night long, these qualities of God which had made the night possible.

"I know, Pammy," I said, hugging her back. "I know."

Still, however far we thought it might be, it was hard to turn our backs to the light and walk once more into the darkness, which, after we had been out of it for a little while, seemed thicker now than ever. Only Pam seemed able to go on with her earlier energy. Jeff had been stumping on his badly wounded leg since the middle of the afternoon. It was clear he was reaching the limits of his physical endurance, though Pam walked on beside him offering what assistance she could. I had no injury like Jeff's, yet I had been exhausted from traveling when I left from home. Limping along behind them, I realized clearly that we were very close to reaching the bridge and the road over; still I was so tired I was nauseated. In spite of Pam's encouraging words, I could hardly imagine how I was going to have the strength to ford the river in the dark, hike some more without being able to see my feet, then climb the high bank that led up to the bridge.

Stumbling along behind them, for a long time, I could hear Jeff and Pam murmuring to each other ahead of me as they looked for a place on the river that would be shallow and well-lit enough to walk through safely.

I trusted my friends, but I couldn't bring myself to trust the spot they picked out for our fording. The water into which we were to step seemed to me to be as broad as a pond. It was opaque beneath our feet, too, its flat surface shimmering faintly from the distant light on the bridge down the river. Though the mud and grasses at its edge and the absence of slope to its bank suggested it was shallow, I worried about one of us stepping off and being swallowed up in a deep hole.

In spite of my fears, we had no problem with the crossing itself. We linked arms as we went in, Jeff between Pam and me. She and I measured the depth of the water in front of us and braced ourselves with the paddles as we inched forward. Though we were prepared for trouble, the bottom was smooth and sandy, and at no place did the water reach above the middle of our legs. Still, it took a long time to get across to the farther bank.

Once across, we stopped for a minute or two to catch our breath and shake the water off our bodies like dogs; then we headed immediately through the marshy terrain to the long, high bank leading to the bridge.

The rest of the way, in clear sight of salvation, so to speak, should have been psychologically easy. For me, at least, it wasn't. Having come this far, I found the climb to the top of the very steep hill very nearly impossible. Ready to fall down in my tracks with exhaustion, I had long since forgotten I had expected to die on the river that night; the results of my peaceful though painful ruminations on my past, death, and time were gone from my memory entirely.

By now, I was blind and deaf with weariness, but there was nothing to do but go up. In a poor imitation of a human being moving on two feet, I began the ascent at the bottom of the bank. I attempted to use the paddle by sticking it into the ground in front of me and pulling myself up with it, but within a foot or two of climbing, it was apparent even to me that this was not about to work. The last time I fell, I gave up, rolled myself over onto my hands and knees, and whining and whimpering in a way I hadn't even been tempted to before, began to crawl forward and slip back, crawl forward and slip back, through the mud, rocks, grass, and briars of that impossible but well-lit hill.

Crawling up the hill, it seems to me now, I had been

reduced at last to no more than a crying, self-centered bundle of physical needs and desires. Knowing how hard Jeff had to be struggling behind me as he dragged his injured leg behind him, I was even then ashamed of my sniveling, but I sniveled, slithering and bumping along in my extremity, nonetheless. Concerned only with myself—may God, Jeff, and Pam forgive me—I knew it and I hated what I felt I had come to.

I climbed on like that forever, it seemed to me, until at last, neck bent, eyes fixed only on the ground before me, I put my hand out into what should have been the stony dirt of the hill above me. Half dead, covered from head to toe in mud, bits of leaves, and various kinds of seeds and stickers, I had come to the top; I was at the road.

Somehow, I pulled myself upright and looked over the side of the hill to check on the progress of my companions below me. They, too, were nearly to the top. I was overwhelmed with relief.

"Pam, Jeff," I called out to them. "I'm here! Come on up; you just have a little more to go."

There was a little grunting and muttering; then Jeff answered. "What time is it?" he asked.

I pushed up the sleeve on my raincoat to see. Though the light had been bright enough to illumine my watch for some time now, probably for the first time in my life I had forgotten to look at it when I had the chance.

"Six-thirty!" I said, amazed. "It's six-thirty." I had thought it couldn't have been much past midnight.

"Really?" Jeff asked, and Pam echoed him, "Are you sure?"

I glanced up. Now I could see that, though the sun was

nowhere visible, the sky was indeed beginning to glow a nearly electric blue.

"Really," I said.

By the time the three of us were standing side by side on the highway at the end of the bridge, daylight was well on its way and I was frantic to let Richard know that we were all right. In desperate need of a ride to the van, we stuck out our thumbs at the first two cars that approached us. As they got near enough to spot our filthy clothes and faces, leaf-filled hair, and wooden canoe paddles, sensibly they sped up and drove on past.

The third vehicle to approach us was a pickup truck. Being in rural Georgia as we were, my heart pounded in terror as it began to slow down. I was so busy looking for a gun rack on the back window that it was a moment before I could hear the driver's friendly voice speaking to us.

"Boy, do you ever look like you need a ride somewhere," he said. "Hop on in the cab and I'll give you one."

It was then that I noticed how fancy what he was driving was. It was the truck every young man dreams of owning in our part of the country—tall, two-toned, brand-new and shiny with tan and cream paint, chrome hubcaps, and a perfectly clean, unscratched mud liner in the back of it. There was no way we could ride in that cab without scratching and staining everything we touched. It would take hours to clean up after us.

"We'll wreck your truck if we do," I said.

"That's okay," he answered. "You look like you need all the help you can get." We haggled awhile until he agreed that we would climb into the open back; at least he could hose it out later without much damage.

We climbed in at last, Jeff struggling to raise himself up with his bad knee. We huddled in the cold air at the front to talk to the driver through the window as he took us to the gas station to call Richard before we went on to the van.

Through the rushing wind and into the open window, where the gun rack would have been if there had been one, we shouted the story of our adventures and Jeff's injury. He told us he had been on the way to work in the mall when he saw us and stopped for us. We said we were infinitely grateful, and we hoped he wouldn't lose his job for being late. He answered that he doubted that he would, and besides, he couldn't have left us there; what else could he have done?

Overcome by humility, gratitude, and wonder at the spontaneous generosity this man was showing us, I almost didn't notice when we pulled up at the service station, which, it being seven o'clock, was just opening for the day.

A moment later, I was dialing the pay phone by the door.

My husband picked it up at his end on the first ring.

"Richard," I said, "is that you?"

"Sweetie?" he answered, his voice cracking with relief. "You're alive! Where are you? Are you all right? I've been planning the funeral service since four o'clock."

Whatever he'd been doing, I was so glad to hear his voice I was weak-kneed. I would have sat down if there had been a place to sit.

"I haven't known what to do," he went on. "The police came out to the house about eleven and told me I shouldn't worry about you: wives just run off sometimes, and besides, you were probably only out shopping with your friends. I called the Game and Fish Division about one o'clock, and they scared me to death. The woman on the desk said you were on the most dangerous stretch of the Flint River she knew. Last night was the first night of deer hunting and wild boar rutting season, besides. They would send their people in to look for you, but not before daylight. It was just too risky. In fact," he added," I've got to call them right away before they send out the helicopters."

Leaving out the more terrifying parts, quickly I told him some of what had actually happened to us and when we thought we would be back home; then I hung up. Our new friend took us back out into the countryside where we'd left the van near the deer carcass in the ditch. We thanked him profusely and he went on to work while we drove to the car, which Pam was to take back to Atlanta.

By nine o'clock, Richard was stripping off my ruined clothes and dropping them on the black and white tile floor of our bathroom. Steam from the shower filled the room, and the bed, which he had not slept in the night before, was turned back and waiting.

Happy as I was to see him, I could tell he was almost beside himself from the strain of what he had been through. His eyes had the sunken look they get when he has a migraine, and he had red patchy places at the tops of his cheeks. A few minutes later he stopped picking the leaves and twigs out of my hair to hug me again.

"I thought you were dead," he whispered.

"I thought so, too," I whispered back. "Give me a little bit, and I'll tell you what it was like."

That, except for the immediate mop-up, was the end of the actual events surrounding our adventure on the Flint River. The canoe was gone for good; none of us would have returned to fetch it if it had cost a thousand dollars. Richard was emotionally exhausted, suffered from stomachaches, and looked terrible around the eyes for a good two weeks. For a long time, he and I were clingy and overprotective of each other.

The three of us who had been out all night got tetanus shots and took antibiotics. Jeff and Pam, who had both been wearing canvas shoes, lost some toenails. (I had been shod in leather; though my moccasins had to be thrown away, my feet were intact.) For two weeks at least, all of us were covered with bruises and, in spite of the anti-inflammatories, bent double with sore back, arm, and shoulder muscles. After three weeks of severe pain, Jeff had knee surgery.

It wasn't only our bodies that needed tending to, either. We all had nightmares, and something oddly like daymares as well; each of us found that for a good while afterward, every time we closed our eyes we saw pictured on our eyelids black, leaf-filled water, vines, and snakes, and we had trouble catching our breath. I didn't tell my mother of any of it for two years—why should she have that worry?—but we explained compulsively to everyone else what had happened that night, to incredulous friends and polite colleagues, to people we didn't even know in the checkout line at the grocery store, to the mailman, to distant neighbors, and to anyone else who was willing to listen.

Considering everything, it wouldn't seem to me to be much of an aftermath to our adventure if this were the whole of it, but of course, it wasn't the whole of it. Living through it at the time and reflecting and praying over it later, I learned more than I would ever have thought I could learn. Like Julian of Norwich in the illness that laid her low when she was thirty and a half years old, from before the time I ever left home I had reason to believe that I would die on that trip, and I had continued to believe it until the very time we came to the place where we forded the river. Throughout the night I had examined myself, prepared for death, and, through the grace of renunciation in the presence of God, faced loss and my past failures and held myself in readiness for it. I learned from all of it, even from the end when I collapsed in a heap, concerned only with myself, no longer believing I would die.

From the beginning, I began to learn of death, both that it is not so fearsome as I'd thought since childhood and that God is with us, fully present in it and to it, in ways I had not before imagined. (As a theologian, shouldn't I have known this already from the very fact of God's own death in the incarnation, which I profess? Yes, of course, I should have, but I didn't.)

I saw God's Word, the same one who was made flesh in Jesus Christ of Nazareth. I heard that Word speaking in the wilderness, a shining star in darkness, the very light and truth, structure and goodness that sustains the world, and it was the same Word, coming out of my own mouth and shining in my friend.

I glimpsed, and ruminate still, over the backside of the God I can never fully know, through whose eyes I can never see, but who I now know hates the suffering and death of human beings in ways too deep for me, whose kindness and generosity are unfathomable. I understood then, and I understand now in my very bones, that this is the God about whom no one can ever say, "I will tell you with certainty that if you think these things, believe these words, or break these laws, you will be cast out of God's presence forever."

I experienced and have continued to mull over God's twin gifts of gratitude and renunciation that not only kept me alive that night, but made me supple, open to love and to be loved, ready in that present to receive with a certain kind of joy every single thing that came to me. What came to me as gifts I cultivate humbly now, however I am able, as demanding and happy disciplines of God.

From Pam and from a stranger in a pickup truck I learned more deeply than ever that all human kindness, generosity, compassion, and goodness belong to the heart of the image of God in which we are made, and as God is unknowable, so too, are these virtues, even in their capacity to heal and enliven, unlimited and unknowable.

I came, too, to know far better than I did before—are we all already aware of this at some level we do not choose to acknowledge?—that to have to turn back and walk into the dark woods when the destination is in sight, even to slide down a hill in despair without an ounce of mindfulness or compassion, does not mean I will not reach my goal in God if only I hang on and am persistent.

Finally, I came to know for myself, though I don't understand it still, that in the time of this beloved God, death has surely been defeated, and all creation—all human beings, all sentient life, all dear ones, Douglas, Pam, my mother and father, Richard, my grandparents, my distant teachers of the desert, every memory and every story, each rock and each river, angels, cats, babies, old women and men, children—all are held in being, healed, cherished in some mysterious way, and nourished on the invisible body and blood of Christ in the eternal now of God.

Reader, for all these gifts of the Flint River, as for every good gift, I thank God now with gratitude and love. I ask God for help as I continue to ponder them and keep them close. I offer my prayers for you, that you also may find gifts in your own experience of wilderness.